In Loving Memory
THE STORY OF
UNDERCLIFFE CEMETERY

COLIN CLARK & REUBEN DAVISON

SUTTON PUBLISHING

Sutton Publishing Limited
Phoenix Mill · Thrupp · Stroud
Gloucestershire · GL5 2BU

First published 2004

British Library Cataloguing in Publication Data
A catalogue record for this book is available from the
British Library.

ISBN 0-7509-3673-8

Title page photograph: A fragment from a
porcelain grave ornament found in the
undergrowth during the restoration of the
cemetery. (*Authors' collection*)
Below: This is a common motif to be found
on gravestones in the cemetery, commonly
made of porcelain The motif of clasped
hands represents friendship and farewell.
(*Authors' collection*)

Typeset in 10.5/13.5 Photina.
Typesetting and origination by
Sutton Publishing Limited.
Printed and bound in England by
J.H. Haynes & Co. Ltd, Sparkford.

This book is dedicated to all those people who, in many
different ways, helped and supported the efforts to preserve
Undercliffe Cemetery. But the biggest debt is to the handful of
volunteers, local men who every day give their time and effort
to keep the place going: to Barry (in the early days), Joe, Jack,
Graham, George, Charlie and the 'other' John, for all your time
and effort – we salute you!

CONTENTS

LORD MAYOR'S FOREWORD

I was delighted to be asked by Colin and Reuben to write a foreword for this splendid book on the nationally famous Undercliffe Cemetery. The 25-acre burial ground at Undercliffe is without doubt one of the country's finest nineteenth-century cemeteries and a wonderful collection of some of the finest examples of High Victorian funerary art.

The photographs in this book vividly bring to life the stunning architectural grandeur of the cemetery and the wealth of fascinating social history which lies behind the stones. Many of those who were instrumental in the growth of Victorian Bradford were laid to rest within the confines of the cemetery, reflecting in death the burgeoning, wealthy place the town had become.

The dark days of the 1970s and the early 1980s saw the cemetery tragically lose all its buildings and become an overgrown wilderness. Happily, in recent years its

glories – once dimmed through neglect and lack of interest – have been re-discovered and restored and are now being appreciated by a whole new generation of admirers. We are perhaps coming full circle in this: re-establishing the nineteenth-century ethos of the cemetery as a place of recreation and quiet contemplation, though now with the added incentive of being able to discover there so much about the historical development of our City and our forebears.

Colin and Reuben have put together a wonderful book which I, for one, will return to with pleasure time and again and I congratulate them on their painstaking work and diligent research.

Councillor Allan Irving Hillary
Lord Mayor of Bradford 2003–4

INTRODUCTION

I have been involved with Undercliffe Cemetery for the last twenty-three years almost on a daily basis, firstly campaigning to save it and then looking after the site, so I was delighted to collaborate with Reuben when he appeared out of the blue and said he wanted to produce a book about the cemetery. We did not intend it to be an intellectual work on Victorian social history, funeral customs or monumental architecture. There are many volumes by people who are far better able to produce works of a more academic nature. Our intention is to put together the story of one cemetery using illustrations, some never published before, with just enough text to join the whole thing together.

This book is loosely based on the illustrated talk I have been giving for many years to interested groups and societies – the founding of the original Bradford Cemetery Company, its role in Bradford's Victorian society, its eventual demise and near destruction through ignorance, apathy and neglect; then the fight to save it by the 'Friends' and its ultimate restoration and rebirth as a beautiful and useful asset to the city and its people under the care of the 'Undercliffe Cemetery Charity'.

As time goes by the very circumstances which caused its downfall could occur again and this historic treasure of Bradford's history, culture and architectural heritage might be finally lost to posterity. I hope this book will in some small way help to prevent this; if not then we will at least have a record of what we have lost!

Colin Clark

My involvement with this book came about following my return to Bradford after eight years away. I knew of the 1980s campaign to restore the cemetery to its former glory and also took many photographs during the late seventies. When I tried to find out what, if anything, was happening at the cemetery it was Colin who explained the situation to me. My work prevented me from offering practical daytime help with grounds maintenance, but being employed by a publisher of local history titles I thought a book would not only raise awareness of the cemetery but would also collate the wealth of available but unpublished information.

Undercliffe Cemetery is a magnificent site. A walk to the western end of the promenade rewards the visitor with a stunning panorama across the city. The people of Bradford should be proud of the cemetery and the people buried there, for, as local historian Alfred Robinson said of Undercliffe, 'This is indeed Bradford's history in stone.'

Reuben Davison

SOME COMMON MISCONCEPTIONS CORRECTED

It is true that Robert Milligan was the first Mayor of Bradford (when it was incorporated in 1847) but *not* that he was the first Lord Mayor – this was actually John Arthur Godwin.

Of the architectural firm Mawson & Lockwood, only *Mawson* is buried in Undercliffe. His partner Lockwood lies in a Leeds cemetery; the Lockwood whose grave is opposite Mawson's was a laundry manager.

The first burial in Undercliffe is commonly believed to have been on 25 July 1854, but this was in the consecrated section; the *first actual* burial was in the cemetery's unconsecrated section on 10 March 1854.

Although Sir Titus Salt was on the first board of directors he built his own mausoleum at Saltaire and was interred there, *not* at Undercliffe.

The present-day Lodge at the Undercliffe Lane entrance was *not* moved from Bowling Cemetery but came from the entrance to the Mitchell estate on Rooley Lane.

It is *not* a misconception that maps of Bradford fail to show Undercliffe Cemetery, except as Bradford Cemetery. Since the local authority, the Ordnance Survey and other mapmakers have not amended their data in the last fifty years, it can be difficult for prospective visitors to find the cemetery.

SYMBOLISM IN FUNERARY ART

anchor: hope, or being 'at rest'

book: with a cross on – faith

columns: complete – a full life; broken – a life cut short

crown: the emblem of a Christian martyr who will find reward in heaven

hourglass: traditional symbol of time

IHS: *Iesus Hominum Salvator* – Jesus Saviour of Mankind

ivy: an evergreen – immortality or friendship

lamp: immortality; a light to heaven

laurel: fame – usually as a wreath, often on graves of artistic people

lily: purity

lion: courage, strength, resurrection

oak leaves: victory

palm: triumph, or a martyr's death

obelisk: eternal life, taken from Egyptian sun-worshipping symbols

phoenix: Christ's resurrection

rocks: the Church, or Christian steadfastness

rose: usually a lack of sin

scythe: the passage of time and death

shell: a pilgrimage to heaven

ship: the Christian Church carrying the faithful through the world

snake: with its tail in its mouth, eternity

sundial: the passage of time

torch: immortality; if upturned, a life cut short

urn: draped and empty – death; flaming – new life

weeping fig: grief, like willow or yew

wheat: fruitfulness harvested.

1

In the Beginning

A view of Bradford by John William Anderson (1792–1851), painted a dozen years
before Victoria came to the throne. The artist's viewpoint must have been
somewhere at the western end of the cemetery.
(*Courtesy of Bradford City Art Galleries & Museums*)

Be sure to lay me there, he said,
In that sweet lovely spot
And strew with flowers my grassy bed
To prove I'm not forgot.

Memorial to Henry Parker 1871
Beckett Street Cemetery, Leeds

The country which destroys its past deserves to have no future.

Winston Churchill

To walk firmly into the future you need to know about the past.

At the beginning of the nineteenth century the industrial revolution was well under way. The agrarian and cottage industry economy was changing to the steam-driven mills and mass production of the factories. The emerging industrial centres were greedy for labour and in the rural areas country folk, often desperate for work, made a bee-line for the developing cities. Some, such as Robert Milligan, migrated to Bradford from Dumfries as a lad and found fame and fortune, becoming Bradford's first Mayor in 1847, but for many it was a hard and short life!

This migration to the towns created enormous problems of housing and sanitation. Health and safety was not considered of major importance and life in the factories was exhausting and often dangerous. Epidemics such as cholera and scarlet fever spread rapidly, giving an average life span of 17 for the working classes and 34 for the 'gentry'. Many did live to a great age but it was the appalling infant mortality rate that brought these averages down.

Along with the high mortality rate Bradford wasn't a 'clean' town by any stretch of the imagination. James Smith in his report for the Health of Towns Commission in 1844 concluded: 'of Bradford I am obliged to pronounce it the most filthy town I have visited'. He described it as having 'courts, yards and privies, open cesspits, pig styes and slaughterhouses and effluent laden watercourses'.

If you had been born in Bradford up to the middle of the nineteenth century you would have been baptised, married and subsequently buried in the parish church,

The reason why. By the middle of the nineteenth century the parish churches and chapels of the town could not accommodate any more burials. Indeed, many had been struggling for some time to find space. Action had to be taken to find a more hygienic and seemly way of burying the dead. (*Tony Hodgson*)

St Peter's, now the cathedral. Those of the nonconformist faiths had their own chapels and burial grounds within the town. In 1801 Bradford was no more than a market town with a population of around 13,000, and the burial grounds within the limits of the town were able to dispose of the dead adequately. By 1841 the population had grown to 103,000 and disposal of the dead was becoming a major problem.

In 1837 an observer noted that the churchyard was now 'decently full', but its use continued and they managed to pack another few thousand bodies into the grounds. As the mortality rate increased things were coming to crisis point and the concept of cemeteries started to be looked at again. It is worth noting here the difference between a cemetery and a graveyard: a cemetery is a burial ground unattached to a church. The Romans and Saxons had used this method centuries earlier and taken their dead out of the town precinct and buried them in a dedicated area. As Christianity spread the Church steadily took on the role of burial and looked after 'God's little acre'. Since burial constituted a large part of its income the Church did not take too kindly to this cemetery concept.

Finally Government legislation allowed private cemeteries to be established and so the creation began with what the Victorians called the 'Great gardens of sleep'. 'Shall Wakefield, Huddersfield and Halifax excel us? Our pride says nay!' was the plaintive cry of a Bradfordian in a Yorkshire newspaper!

By 1850 Bradford was well overdue for its new commercial cemetery. Many had already been established around the country such as London's Kensal Green and Norwood and the famous Highgate cemetery. A large quarry in Liverpool was landscaped and laid out in 1829. Sheffield people got theirs in the shape of the Central Cemetery in 1836.

Rather belatedly, a group of leading businessmen decided it was time for Bradford to have its cemetery and build this necessary amenity. It shouldn't be forgotten that this was also a business venture designed to make money. It would be several years before the corporation would be allowed to use money from the rates to open municipal cemeteries, Scholemoor being the first in Bradford in 1860.

The Bradford Cemetery Company was provisionally registered in 1849 and received its licence to operate in 1852. Its thirteen directors included such

An original share issue for the Bradford Cemetery Company cost £3 0s 6d. It gradually became known as Undercliffe Cemetery when it ceased to be the only one in Bradford. (*Tony Hodgson*)

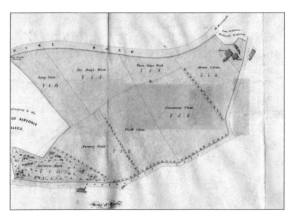

The farmstead and field that comprised lots 13 and 14 when the Hustler estate was auctioned. The new Bradford Cemetery Company made a successful bid of £3,400 for the two lots. (*Authors' collection*)

luminaries as Sir Titus Salt and Robert Milligan, Bradford's first Mayor. A share issue was floated and a suitable site then had to be found.

The criteria were that it was to be of the required acreage, on the outskirts of the town but still have reasonable access. Such a parcel of land became available at Undercliffe when the Hustlers, a wealthy Quaker family, wanted to sell off their estate. Ironically it was described at the time by John Horsfall of the Bradford *Observer* in 1850 as 'a site where the town is least likely to expand to'.

The auction was held at the Sun Inn at the bottom of Ivegate on 16 July 1851 and two lots, 13 and 14, comprising 26 acres of farm land and buildings, were purchased for £3,400. The land was encompassed on the north side by the Otley turnpike and on the south by Undercliffe Lane.

William Gay was commissioned as the designer and John Dale the architect. The cost of the project was to be £12,000 and William Gay had been chosen because he had already earned his reputation with his work at the Leicester cemetery. His design for Undercliffe led to other commissions such as Horton Park and in addition to this work he also agreed to stay on as the company's first registrar.

Having raised the necessary capital and acquired the site, work could start on laying out the grounds and building the Registrar's house and office and the gardener's and sexton's lodges. Two mortuary chapels were also built, one for Anglicans and one for Dissenters. The existing farm buildings on the eastern side of

The Sun Inn, Bradford. This was the centre of commercial and political activity in mid-nineteenth-century Bradford. It stood at the bottom of Ivegate and Sunbridge Road. The auction of the Hustler estate was held here on 16 July 1851. (*Bradford Libraries*)

A poster advertising the sale of the Hustler estate. (*Authors' collection*)

BRADFORD CEMETERY.

CONSECRATION,

FRIDAY, 25th AUGUST, 1854.

ORDER OF PROCESSION

*From the Lodge (Harrogate Road) to the Chapel : and after Divine
Service, from the Chapel on the Ground.*

POLICE.

REGISTRAR OF CEMETERY.

CONTRACTORS.

ARCHITECTS.

DIRECTORS & SHAREHOLDERS.

SECRETARY AND SOLICITORS.

TOWN CLERK AND MEMBERS OF THE TOWN COUNCIL.

MAYOR AND MAGISTRATES.

VERGERS.

CHURCHWARDENS.

CHORISTERS.

VICAR AND READER.

THE BISHOP OF RIPON.

THE ARCHDEACON AND REGISTRAR.

THE CLERGY.

POLICE.

A poster announcing the Consecration ceremony. This was really the official opening, and over 4,000 people attended. (*Authors' collection*)

the cemetery were used as the monumental stone-mason's workshops and dwellings.

Undercliffe was laid out to capture the panoramic views from the western end of the main promenade. Ornamental planting and shrubberies were used to great effect not only to enhance the site but also to screen 'lower-class' graves from the more 'affluent'. The chapels were possibly of wooden construction and designed by architects Mallinson & Healey.

The directors stated in the first publication of the Rule Book in 1854 that 'the present chapels are only temporary erections. Plans for permanent stone buildings of an elegant design are prepared but prudential motives have delayed their being carried out at present.' It is possible that the company needed to have a few more burials and establish a regular cash flow before the grander designs could go ahead.

By 1878 the cemetery company decided more permanent structures were now feasible and employed the architectural firm of Lockwood & Mawson. These chapels dominated the promenade and central core until their demolition in the 1980s.

Cemetery design considered not only efficient use of space – fitting in the maximum number of plots – but also followed aesthetic guidelines as well. They were designed like parks, an area to be visited on a Sunday morning to socialise with one's peers.

The grounds were open for burials by March 1854 followed by an official opening ceremony and consecration by the Bishop of Ripon, the Right Revd C.T. Longley, on 28 August 1854, a ceremony attended by over four thousand people. It is interesting to point out as an historical footnote that by the time of the 'official' opening over thirty-one burials had already taken place in the unconsecrated grounds. The person with the dubious honour of being the first burial was Ann Scarf, aged twenty-two years, spinster of Little Horton.

Once the cemetery had been opened a local man wrote to the paper: 'It is a great relief to know we can deposit our earthly remains in such an appropriate place as the one I refer to, with the assurance they will not be rudely disturbed.'

The Directors of the company were aware of the extended use for the cemetery and wrote that 'they desire to throw the cemetery open to the public as much as possible, so long as propriety and behaviour is observed, a place for contemplative retirement'. This statement can be seen as a subtle 'marketing' ploy. So popular were the cemetery grounds in 1854 that the Town Clerk was directed to instruct the Chief Constable to provide a policeman to 'preserve order at the cemetery during Sundays'.

The cemetery was laid out so that, in death as in life, social status could be observed. It can be seen from the plans that the wealthy reserved many plots for their memorials such as the Illingworth mausoleum, covering eighteen plots The less well-off simply had one plot. At the time of opening in 1854 a freehold grave in the most prestigious part of the cemetery would cost 10 guineas, steadily decreasing to £1 1s for an average grave. The more expensive graves were usually bigger and brick-lined, and on the path sides. Part of the licence requirements for the company was to supply burial plots for the poor. These were opened up in the less favourable areas of the cemetery with as many as forty bodies placed in them and then filled in again when they were full, with no headstone. These were generally known as common or pauper graves, although in Undercliffe they were referred to as 'company graves'.

The cemetery was divided into the unconsecrated eastern section and the consecrated western section, each with its own mortuary chapel. The consecrated ground covers a larger area than the unconsecrated but Bradford had a very large nonconformist population and eventually the unconsecrated grounds had to be extended into the consecrated area. In what is known as the 'Historic Core' too the separation is maintained and it is the unconsecrated ground that has the more prestigious monuments, such as those of the Illingworths and the Holdens, both staunch Methodist families.

In 1855 the Society of Friends (Quakers) purchased 197 plots following the closure of their burial grounds when the land at Goodmans End (bottom of Wakefield Road) was sold to the railway company. These are notable by the fact that the stones lay flat and not upright – 'no man being above another'.

Nearly all of Bradford's prominent families have had some representation in the cemetery. As mentioned earlier, one of the most striking memorials is that of Alfred Illingworth, but along with him are the tombs of Daniel Illingworth, Henry Illingworth and his son Baron Albert Holden Illingworth of Denton and that of Percy Illingworth. But there is no doubt which family member made the greatest impression. With a family fortune made in the local textile industry Alfred could afford to indulge in something spectacular! His mausoleum is in the form of an Egyptian mastaba which is 'an underground burial chamber with room above, i.e. ground level, to store offerings'. This is considered to be the showpiece of the cemetery.

William Mawson of the architectural partnership of Mawson &

William Gay (1814–93). William Gay's modest grave lies just off the main promenade. (*Authors' collection*)

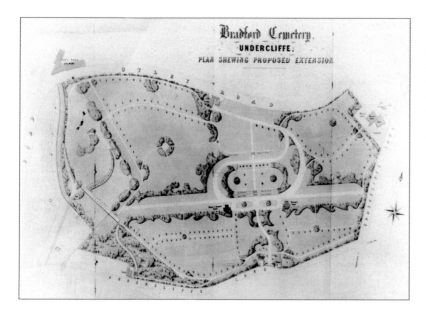

William Gay's plan, as amended in 1876 to show the proposed extension to the western end of the site (Airedale College). This was never achieved and left William Gay very embittered. (*Authors' collection*)

Lockwood, who built the later chapels at Undercliffe, also came to be buried here and his memorial can be seen on the main promenade with his portrait on a bronze plaque. This partnership was also responsible for St George's Hall, the Town Hall and Salt's Mill at Saltaire.

The cemetery plan shows very clearly the central core, where the great wool barons and other wealthy people were interred. From here the cemetery radiates out to the boundaries where the less well-off could afford a plot. The prime position was always beside a path where one could 'be seen'.

Undercliffe Cemetery contains an incredible array of people and professions: Mayors and Lord Mayors, wool barons, MPs, surgeons and clergymen and many thousands of ordinary folk who toiled through life's ups and downs found their last resting place in Undercliffe.

The *Bradford Observer* commented in 1854:

Most large towns have a cemetery to which strangers are taken, not only as being the resting place of 'the mighty dead' but as being one of the most striking and beautiful features of the town to which it belongs.

The reader who has visited Sheffield, Liverpool, Leicester, Hull, Norwich, Edinburgh or Glasgow, will remember with what pride his friend escorted him to the cemetery in those towns and with what volubility they discoursed by the way of the beauties of the place.

Well, we too have a cemetery and one that will vie with the most distinguished we have named for beauty. In extent it is about 25 acres. It is tastefully laid out and will be planted and kept in such a manner as is best adapted to the locality. In the meanwhile, the view of the surrounding country from various points of the grounds is not to be surpassed in the neighbourhood of Bradford.

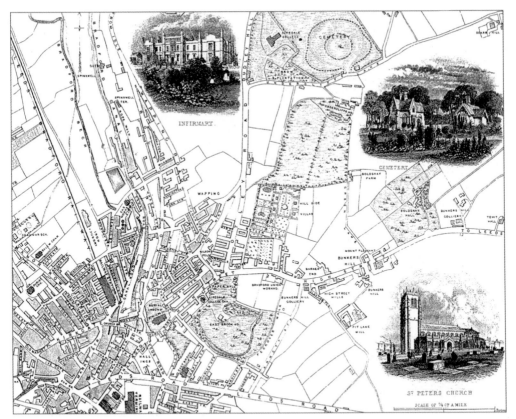

John Tallis's plan of Bradford, published in about 1851. This is the first map to show a cemetery at Undercliffe. At the time the map was drawn William Gay had not yet planned the layout of the cemetery so the map-maker, aware that the land had been sold for this purpose, drew on his imagination, depicting what a cemetery might look like. (*Bradford Libraries*)

Vignette showing the Undercliffe Lane entrance to the cemetery, with the Registrar's house and sexton's lodge more accurately depicted. (*Bradford Libraries*)

This engraving of *c.* 1853 shows a proposed (but not built) development of middle-class villas at Undercliffe. They surround the Hustler mansion, centre foreground, and the Victoria Gardens behind. From left to right behind the houses runs Undercliffe Lane. The road on the right-hand bottom corner became Undercliffe Street. In the middle distance is the site of the cemetery with paths and drives. The cemetery was under construction at this time. The long church-like structure in the centre is artistic licence. This imagined view is looking north across to Baildon Moor, with Ilkley Moor beyond. In the dip to the left is the Aire valley, where Salt's Mill chimney can be picked out. (*West Yorkshire Archives*)

The townspeople flocked to the cemetery on Sundays to socialise and be 'seen'. Compare this mid-century view of Bradford with the earlier Anderson painting. The intervening decades had seen much expansion of the mills and poor quality housing in the town. (*Bradford Libraries*)

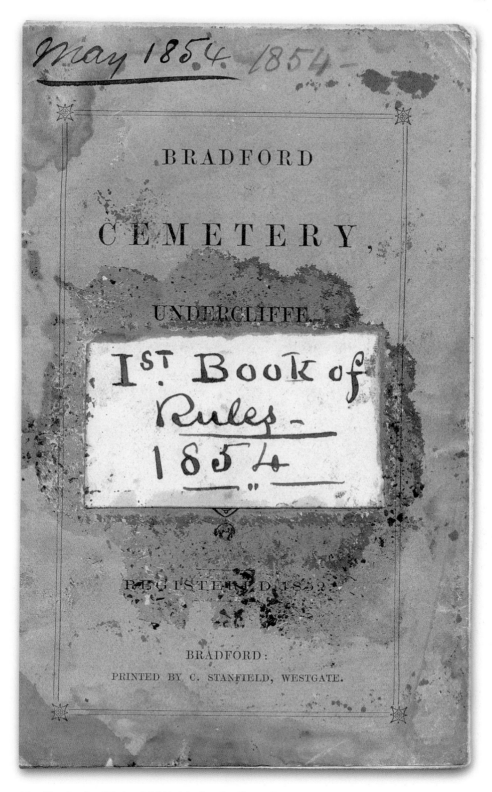

The '1st book of Rules 1854'. (*Authors' collection*)

Joseph Smith (1800–58). He was a
land agent and surveyor.
(*Bradford Libraries*)

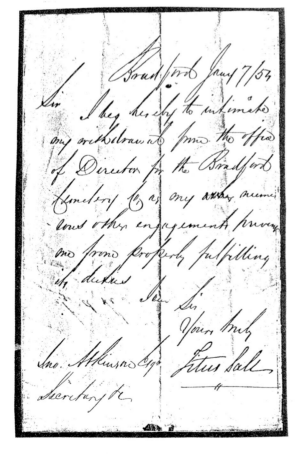

Sir Titus Salt was a founder member
of the Bradford Cemetery Company
but resigned from the Board of
Directors before his name was printed
in the first book of cemetery rules and
regulations. (*West Yorkshire Archives*)

Joseph Smith overlaid the artistic landscape design by William Gay with a grid system to identify the thousands of graves. He chose the most prominent situation at the end of the promenade for his own grave and memorial – the obelisk, which dominates its neighbours. (*Authors' collection*)

CEMETERY DIRECTORS, 1854.

S. SMITH, Esq., Chairman.

A. HARRIS, Jun., Esq., Vice Chairman.

Henry Brown, Esq.	James Keighley, Esq.
Thomas Buck, Esq.	William Rand, Esq.
W. Cheesebrough, Esq.	William Rouse, Esq.
W. Garnett, Esq.	Geo. Rogers, Esq.
John Horsfall, Esq.	I. Wright, Esq.

Secretary.

John Atkinson, Esq.

Treasurer.

S. Laycock, Esq., Bradford Banking Company.

Solicitors.

Messrs. Rawson, George, & Wade.

Registrar.

Mr. William Gay.

Messrs Smith, Brown and Rand were all, at various times, Mayors of Bradford. (*Authors' collection*)

An early photograph of the cemetery looking back to the Undercliffe Lane entrance. The building on the left is the cemetery office and Registrar's house. The two monuments on the right do not now exist and were probably monumental display pieces. (*Bradford Libraries*)

In 1853 a committee of gentlemen, some the founders of Undercliffe Cemetery, purchased the Bolton House estate and established Peel Park for the benefit of the townspeople. This contemporary view of the concourse shows a great similarity with the promenade in Undercliffe Cemetery. This is not surprising because William Gay was the designer of both. The cemetery promenade would have looked very much like this before it was lined with graves and monuments. (*Authors' collection*)

The promenade in Undercliffe Cemetery seen on a postcard of *c.* 1908. (*Courtesy of Graham Hall collection*)

This amateur photograph taken in about 1905 shows the area facing Otley Road where most of the modern-day graves are situated. Owing to problems with the ground it was not opened for burials until 1959. The posing figure may be the head gardener. (*Authors' collection*)

Airedale College, which was moved from Idle to Undercliffe in 1831. When it was demolished in the 1870s the Bradford Cemetery Company's proposal to purchase the site and extend the western end of the cemetery came to nothing and streets of terraced houses were built. Smooth-faced stone blocks (ashlar) from the demolished college can be seen in some of the houses. (*Bradford Libraries*)

An artist's impression of the main concourse looking west. Airedale College was beyond and to the right of the furthest monument. (*Illustrated Weekly News*)

Note the bronze door on the Illingworth tomb, one of the early casualties when the cemetery was abandoned. (*Mark Kilburn*)

An aerial view of the cemetery, mid-1970s. All the buildings are still intact and the paths and drives are clearly visible. The right-hand chapel is the Anglican one and on the left the Dissenters'. The cemetery greenhouses can still be seen in the bottom centre. (*C.H. Wood Photographers*)

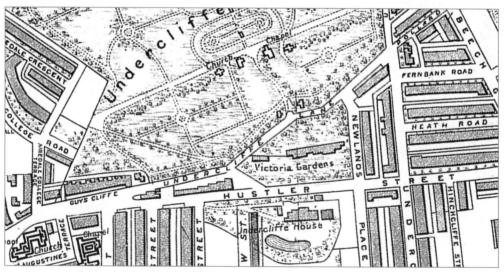

This plan unusually shows two churches and two chapels so it must have been drawn after the Lockwood & Mawson buildings were finished and just before the two cruciform temporary structures were demolished. Across Undercliffe Lane are the Victoria Gardens, apparently a sort of people's park or allotments. Further down the hill is the Hustler mansion. (*Bradford Libraries*)

Opposite: The twin mortuary chapels (Anglican and Dissenters) stood on the main concourse overlooking the 'historic core'. Photographic records of these buildings are rare and only a glimpse is available in this picture. (*Bradford Libraries*)

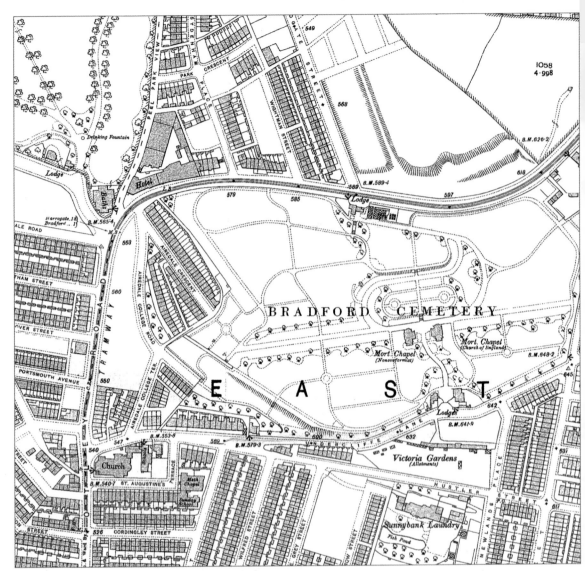

In this plan (*c.* 1908) Airedale College has gone and is replaced by rows of terraced houses. The original concept of placing the cemetery beyond the built-up areas of the town for aesthetic and health reasons only lasted twenty-five years and the site is now almost surrounded by housing. (*Bradford Libraries*)

2

Dereliction

The ornate bronze door of the Holden family monument on the promenade has been ripped out. The urn in the foreground has been knocked off a nearby monument. (*Authors' collection*)

In 1976 the Bradford Cemetery Company went into liquidation. Throughout the twentieth century the number of burials declined to the extent that they could not be commercially viable. It was offered to the local authority in the hope that they would take it on as a Council cemetery but the proposal fell on stony ground. It was felt that they had enough burial grounds to look after and since the historical and architectural value of Undercliffe Cemetery was apparently lost on that particular generation of councillors and planners, it was put in the hands of liquidators to dispose of in any way possible.

On the day the cemetery directors locked up the cemetery office, complete with all the records, and walked away, the grounds were left open to an orgy of destruction, vandalism and takeover by glue-sniffers, drug-users, fly-tippers and thieves. Paths became overgrown and inaccessible, it became a 'no-go' area for decent folk and yet, remarkably and sadly, people with family plots were still burying their loved ones among the desecrated graves.

The situation became even worse. After two years the liquidator disposed of the entire cemetery – 25 acres, 23,000 graves, five standing buildings and the last resting place of over 123,880 Bradfordians – to a property developer for £5! The developer publicly stated that the cemetery was now 'in safe hands'. Over the next three years, however, all the buildings disappeared, as did many sections of the fabric of the site, and eventually grave surrounds (kerbstones) were removed by the hundreds. This remarkable and irreplaceable collection of funerary art and architecture, together with thousands of more modest graves, was now a litter-strewn wilderness.

The Undercliffe Lane entrance. After the cemetery company abandoned the site it did not take long for the lodges to be attacked by thieves and vandals. Eventually both buildings, the sexton's house on the left and cemetery office on the right, were demolished for the value of the stone, leaving piles of debris. (*Authors' collection*)

The rubble-strewn entrance. (*Authors' collection*)

The entrance and lodge today. (*Authors' collection*)

The neglected promenade before the demolition of the chapels. *(Telegraph & Argus)*

Vandalised monuments in the overgrown historic core. *(Authors' collection)*

A machine moves in to demolish the Otley Road lodge, simply for the value of the stone – £650! *(Telegraph & Argus)*

Looking down to the Otley Road entrance. The gatehouse has gone. The area in the fore-ground was the site of the cemetery's three greenhouses. *(Authors' collection)*

The Holden monument on the promenade became a glue-sniffers' den. (*Authors' collection*)

Crosses were an easy target for the destructive actions of vandals. (*Authors' collection*)

Precarious pinnacles. The Swithin Anderton monument. (*Authors' collection*)

Many vaults were broken open. (*Authors' collection*)

Many monuments received the unwelcome attention of local 'artists'. The disturbed top is not the result of vandalism, however. It was dislodged by the branch of a tree, and has been in this position for over twenty years. (*Authors' collection*)

A fallen angel. (*Authors' collection*)

The Garnett memorial in the historic core became the last resting place of a supermarket trolley. And 'Milly' left her mark here as she did in many places around the cemetery. *(Telegraph & Argus)*

A tip-off to the *Telegraph & Argus* one morning brought staff photographer Dennis Flatt up to the cemetery to photograph the wholesale destruction and desecration by the then 'owner'. His visit was not welcomed so he retired to a safe distance and got out his telephoto lens. On that day alone three loads of kerbstones (grave stones) were removed and taken to a local stone yard. (*Telegraph & Argus*)

Kerbstones stacked up ready for removal. (*Authors' collection*)

Many headlines on the plight of the cemetery appeared in the Bradford *Telegraph & Argus* but none more telling than those seen here. (*Telegraph & Argus*)

3

Restoration & Rebirth

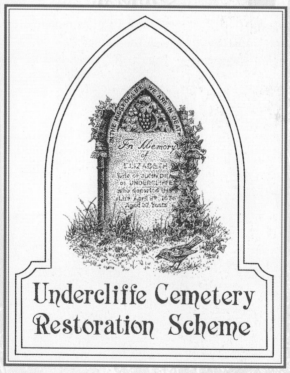

Undercliffe Cemetery Restoration Scheme

The restoration scheme logo. The start of the council-sponsored restoration scheme received a high media profile. It was a pioneering scheme and led to other local authorities taking seriously the future of their neglected Victorian cemeteries. Bradford led the way, (and as a result many threatened burial grounds are now conserved.

An early attempt by a local group to do something about the predicament of the cemetery came to nothing. The scale of the problem was beyond their resources but by 1981 more serious efforts were being made to save the site. Letters were appearing in the local newspaper, councillors were lobbied and there was even some TV coverage. In 1980 Ken Powell of the Victorian Society wrote a telling article in *Country Life* called 'Vandals in Valhalla'.

The protests grew and a deputation of councillors and officers at last inspected the site with the owner and a band of angry protestors; this led to the Council holding a public meeting attended by more than three hundred people. The result was the formation of a committee, representing numerous campaign members, to fight for the preservation of Undercliffe Cemetery; thus the Friends of Undercliffe Cemetery were born.

They were doggedly persistent and tireless in their fight. Paul Parker of the Bradford *Telegraph & Argus* became the unofficial press officer and a stream of stories appeared condemning what was going on. After an intense three-year campaign, with the added support and influence of solicitor Roger Suddards CBE, eventually the Council began to take the Friends seriously, and at a full Council meeting in April 1984 a restoration programme was approved.

The cemetery was compulsorily purchased from its then owner (the property developer) and declared a Conservation Area. A public meeting, two exhibitions and much media coverage raised the profile of the cemetery, and in 1985 an extensive work programme began, sponsored by Bradford Council and the Manpower Services

To publicise the restoration two public exhibitions were held, one in a local school and one in the Bradford Central Library. (*Authors' collection*)

Commission. The three-year project was decommissioned after two years, however, and Undercliffe was once again abandoned, with much work unfinished.

The Friends group, having achieved their objectives in saving the cemetery, disbanded and were succeeded by a new organisation, the Undercliffe Cemetery Charity, to administer and look after the site. This was a registered company with a management board and was granted charitable status.

The council were to provide a small annual grant to ensure the Charity could function, and to protect their investment, but this was eventually withdrawn in 1998. Many tasks and challenges faced the new custodians. The Lodge, moved from its original site on Rooley Lane, remained unfinished – as did the car parks – but the largest and most difficult problem was the maintenance of the grounds. Gradually the members took control, grants were obtained, and the car parks and Lodge were finally completed.

With much of the cemetery restored and looking tidy, more burials were taking place and there was an increased demand for new plots. Once again the cemetery was opened up, visitors came from near and far, schools used the cemetery for educational visits, film-makers made the most of the dramatic scenery and atmosphere.

From the first day it was realised that the entire area could not be cleared, and in any case this was not seen as desirable. Nature had claimed back vast areas and it was thought best to leave these for the wildlife. The philosophy was 'gentle restoration'.

This is part of the display at Bradford Central Library. (*Authors' collection*)

Further publicity was gained by producing a series of cemetery postcards, cemetery trails, guidebooks, leaflets and information packs. This one shows an angel and the one below shows Quaker graves. *(Above, Peter Cooper; below, authors' collection)*

Two milestones in the restoration were, first, winning the coveted BBC award for the nationwide competition 'It's My City' in the heritage category, and then in 1998 gaining English Heritage recognition and becoming a listed area. Other minor accolades were awards from 'Keep Britain Tidy' and 'Nature in the Churchyard'.

In the late 1970s and early 1980s all the buildings in the cemetery were demolished, including the sexton's lodge, the Registrar's house, the cemetery office, the head gardener's lodge at the Otley Road entrance along with greenhouses and the two mortuary chapels on the promenade.

When restoration started the Manpower Services/Community Work Programme established their own compound, but once the charity took over it was realised a more permanent building would be required on site. A derelict, roofless building on Rooley Lane was acquired; it had been the lodge house of Joseph and Abraham Mitchell's estate. Joseph is buried in Undercliffe Cemetery (Abraham in Bowling Cemetery) so it seems entirely proper that part of Joseph's estate should follow him to his grave 114 years after his death.

The removal and restoration of the building, overseen by David Moorhouse of Bradford Council, was highly technical and complex. Originally built in the 1860s it had to be reassembled to current building regulations and specifications and be provided with a matching extension for toilets, kitchen and storage. It was opened in 1991 by the then Lord Mayor of Bradford Cllr Sydney Collard, and is now the focal point for the volunteer workforce as well as committee meetings and visiting groups.

Heavy lifting gear had to be brought in to reinstate the larger monuments. *(Telegraph & Argus)*

The restoration team start work on the central historic core. *(Telegraph & Argus)*

Resurfacing the worn out drives and paths and creating car parking facilities were main priorities in the restoration programme. *(Authors' collection)*

The viewing terrace at the western end of the promenade. The retaining wall had previously been removed and had to be made safe. (*Authors' collection*)

A vandalised 'chest tomb' lid is put back in place. (*Authors' collection*)

Gerry Kershaw, resident stonemason on the Friends committee, led the way on the initial restoration of the monuments. Here he is seen doing much-needed remedial work on the Swithin Anderton memorial. *(Telegraph & Argus)*

The Friends of Undercliffe Cemetery seen doing their bit: from left to right, Gerry Kershaw, Richard Dobson and Tony Chapple. (*Telegraph & Argus*)

Left: The Otley Road gatehouse before demolition. (*Authors' collection*)

Opposite: The massive stone steps leading down to the historic core had to be re-set for public safety. (*Authors' collection*)

Left: The Gothic-style gatehouse was the entrance for funerals. The passage under the arch was paved with pitch pine sets to deaden the noise of hooves and carriage wheels as the cortège passed through. The building was used as the head gardener's lodge. (*Authors' collection*)

Opposite: The gatehouse was demolished in 1983, and consequently a new entrance had to be constructed during the restoration of the cemetery. Matching new pillars were built, and the gates were salvaged from a Bradford market and donated by the Bradford Industrial Museum. (*Authors' collection*)

Many of the paths had become overgrown and impenetrable, the monuments hidden from view. (*Authors' collection*)

Under the restoration scheme the shrubbery was cut back and the perimeter paths were edged and resurfaced. This provided better and safer access for visitors. (*Authors' collection*)

Just one of the piles of building material left in front of the Smith obelisk. (*Authors' collection*)

When the council-sponsored Manpower Services programme was closed down with twelve months still to go it left behind huge piles of detritus and building materials. It took the under-resourced new incumbents (the charity) some time to clean everything up. (*Authors' collection*)

The lodge in its original position on Rooley Lane. The lady in the picture is Mrs Christine Chapple, a founder member of the Friends of Undercliffe Cemetery, whose drive and persistence kept alive the campaign to save the site. (*Yorkshire Post*)

The lodge today at the Undercliffe Lane entrance. It was moved stone by stone from its original site. (*Authors' collection*)

First impressions. Improvements to the entrances were a priority to let visitors see that the cemetery was now being looked after. Granite setts from the old City Road railway goods yard were shipped in by their thousands and used to edge all the drives. (*Authors' collection*)

Roger Suddards CBE unveils a memorial stone. *(Telegraph & Argus)*

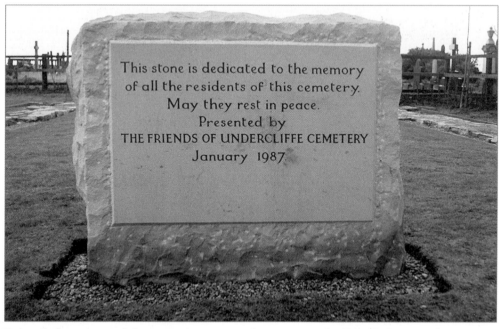

To mark the success of the campaign to save the cemetery the Friends 'presented a stone to commemorate the many thousands of Bradfordians whose eternal sleep had been so rudely disturbed'. Roger Suddards CBE was invited to unveil the memorial. Unfortunately his name was omitted from the inscription, and had to be added later by the stonemason to complete the inscription. *(Authors' collection)*

The Undercliffe Lane entrance reinstated with railings and gates. The cobbled area in the foreground has been stripped of the old tarmacadam coating. (*Authors' collection*)

Undercliffe Cemetery wins heritage award

STAR 29/6/89

YOU'RE the tops! Actor Bill Paterson (right) hands over a major BBC heritage award to Colin Clark, one of the volunteers instrumental in turning a run-down burial ground at Undercliffe into a local tourist attraction.

The project to return the 19th century cemetery – where many of Bradford's rich and famous are buried – to its former glory clinched the joint winner's slot in the tourism/heritage section of the prestigious It's My City competition.

And as well as the ceramic trophy received by Mr Clark at the award ceremony in Manchester, the scheme stands to pick up an expected £2,500 in prize money from section sponsors Allied Lyons.

Now, the people who formed a private company to inject new life into the 26-acre Victorian showpiece after it fell victim to vandalism and neglect, are looking on the cemetery's Open Day on Sunday as one of celebration.

"We are gratified the scheme has come to fruition and been recognised at national level," said Mr Clark. "But while we get the praise,

by Georgina Kuchartschuk

there are the unsung heroes like Employment Training, who have done the work, and Bradford Council, who helped us get the whole thing off the ground."

The three-year restoration programme has involved repair work, creating lawned areas, re-erecting damaged monuments, and re-building a period lodge.

Through the efforts of the company, which consists of representatives from the Friends of Undercliffe Cemetery, Bradford Council, the Pennine Heritage Group and locals, the cemetery now draws scores of visitors intrigued by its history and range of memorials.

The Open Day, to run from 11am to 4pm, will give the public a chance to meet committee members, ask questions and be taken on a guided tour.

TEIA COMMENT 26/6/89

Pride of the city

LESS than a handful of years ago, Undercliffe Cemetery was Bradford's shame thanks to decades of neglect and mismanagement: an overgrown jungle full of vandalised monuments. There were many then who voiced their conviction that it could and should be a showpiece for the city. Some of them had enough determination to do something about it. Last night's award to the Bradford Undercliffe Cemetery Company, joint winner of the tourism/heritage section of the It's My City competition, was well deserved. Warmest congratulations and thanks are due to all those involved in saving the cemetery and demonstrating that there is no such thing as a lost cause.

Many events were happening as the restoration progressed. The newspaper cutting shows the actor Bill Paterson presenting the BBC 'It's My City' award for projects involving heritage to a committee member. (*Telegraph & Argus*)

In 1991 the Lord Mayor of Bradford Cllr Sydney Collard officiated at the official ceremony on completion of the lodge. Left to right: Colin Clark, trustee, the Lady Mayoress and the Lord Mayor with a commemorative plaque. (*Authors' collection*)

As the cemetery improved the grounds were opened up for educational visits by schools. Leaflets and information packs were produced as teaching aids. (*Authors' collection*)

The local branch of the British Legion return for the annual Armistice Day service at the cemetery. The picture shows the 2002 ceremony with the Revd A. Bowerman, curate of St Augustine's Church, Cllr A. Hillary (the present Lord Mayor) and Mrs C. Brook, widow of the late Cyril Brook, British Legion Wrose branch. (*Authors' collection*)

New signs placed at both entrances were an attempt to educate the public on the status of the cemetery. (*Authors' collection*)

The much improved current burial area on the north side of the site. Many families now felt they could come back to tend family plots. (*Authors' collection*)

When restoration began the Friends of Undercliffe Cemetery had to take on responsibility for burials, as did the charity when they took over management from the Friends. Fortunately the cemetery records, Grave Book and Burial Register had been preserved virtually intact. Nevertheless the logistics of putting together the various elements of burials required a steep learning curve for those who took it on. With vast improvements to the site families and funeral directors felt reassured that burials in Undercliffe would again be conducted with dignity. In addition to the reopening of existing family graves there was a demand for new plots. Between 1984 and 2003 the new management have conducted 956 burials and sold over 300 new graves. The picture shows Francis Cooper who, with his father Terry, were engaged as freelance grave diggers for many years. All the graves in Undercliffe have to be dug by hand. It is arduous work which has to be done in all weathers. (*Authors' collection*)

Although monuments were repaired during the restoration scheme many were not and occasional acts of vandalism have damaged others. The volunteer group who look after the cemetery have become experts in restoration, sometimes borrowing the 'high-ab' car-lifting vehicle of SOS Recovery, Marshfields, Bradford, for the heavier jobs. The photograph shows volunteers John Loughlin and Darren Rhodes fixing a broken headstone. (*Authors' collection*)

A snag on the block and tackle is sorted out. (*Authors' collection*)

Even after restoration with the cemetery a conservation area and a listed landscape there were still some acts of vandalism to deal with. There was an attempt to steal the Sphinxes, and it was their sheer weight that defeated the thieves. They could not lift them into the stolen getaway van. The Sphinxes are now securely screwed down. (*Telegraph & Argus*)

The Cemetery Registrar surveys
the results of a local resident's
household clearance dumped
in the Quaker burial area.
(Telegraph & Argus)

A stolen car burnt out on the promenade. *(Telegraph & Argus)*

The restoration scheme called for different levels of maintenance with the main areas kept as neat as resources would allow – but it was never an option to clear the entire 25-acre site. (*Authors' collection*)

Nature reclaimed the site many years ago and much is wilderness now. These areas add to the variety of landscape and wildlife habitat. (*Authors' collection*)

Huge banks of rhododendrons have established themselves over the years. Clearance often reveals monuments not seen for many years. (*Authors' collection*)

Many areas cleared recently soon revert to wilderness. (*Authors' collection*)

4

Listed Monuments

William Mawson (1827–89). Born in Leeds, architect William Mawson moved to Bradford in 1851 when he and his partner Henry Lockwood obtained a commission to build St George's Hall. This was just the start of an illustrious career designing some of Bradford's best known buildings, including Salts Mill, the Great Northern Hotel (1867) subsequently known as the Victoria Hotel, the Wool Exchange (1867, now Waterstone's bookshop), and the Town Hall (1873), a wonderful gothic building with a 220ft tower modelled on the campanile of the Palazzo Vecchio in Florence. Mawson & Lockwood designed the mortuary chapels at Undercliffe that were built in 1878 and finally in 1889 Mawson got his own memorial, an Egyptian obelisk with a fine bronze portrait of William at the base. (*Authors' collection*)

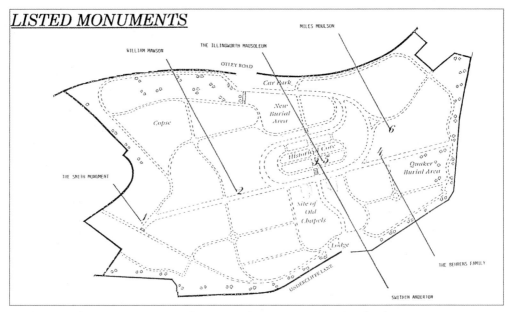

In 1977, when there were serious fears that the cemetery was due for destruction, an attempt was made to get many of the monuments listed. After inspection by the Department of the Environment six were granted listed status: those of Joseph Smith, William Mawson, Swithin Anderton, Sir Jacob Behrens, Alfred Illingworth and Miles Moulson. The plan shows where they are to be found. However, the entire cemetery was designated a Conservation Area in 1984 and in effect the whole site is now 'protected'. In 1998 it was listed by English Heritage in their Register of Parks and Gardens of special historic interest. (*Authors' collection*)

Above left: Miles Moulson (1806–56). Possibly one of the most fitting monuments is that of Miles Moulson who was himself a mason. His memorial is a life-sized female figure standing next to an urn. It was carved by John Throp, a Leeds sculptor. (*Authors' collection*)

Above right: Sir Jacob Behrens. Jacob Behrens, born in Pyrmont, Germany, was another of Bradford's elite engaged in worsted manufacture. Many German families came to Bradford and founded offices and warehouses off Church Bank, so much so that the area became known as Little Germany, a name it retains to this day.

Behrens moved to Bradford in 1838 from Leeds to be, as he put it, 'on the spot'. He not only spent time within his chosen industry but became a fighter for educational reform, founding Bradford High School which he and other businessmen set up primarily for the education of their own sons. The school later became Bradford Grammar School. Behrens was also one of the founder members of the Bradford Chamber of Commerce. You can find the Behrens memorial on the main promenade towards the east side of the cemetery. This ornately decorated 20ft-high construction is in the Baroque Tablet style, and commemorates various members of the Behrens family. The Behrens family remain in the textile business and some years ago had the memorial stone cleaned and returned to its former glory. The pun is prominent in heraldic design and the Behrens monument uses it to the full extent. The most obvious is the bear shown standing on one hind leg. Above this are two six-pointed stars, or mullets, and in between them a bee with its wings outspread. The bee could be interpreted as standing for the 'B' in Behrens or could relate to the idea of the business as in 'busy bee'. (*Authors' collection*)

Opposite, below: Swithin Anderton (1804–60). Swithin Anderton was a JP and wool-stapler and Bradford's first so-called 'wool baron'. His monument is magnificent. It stands in the area known as the historic core and dominates that particular part of the cemetery. It resembles a scaled-down version of the Albert Memorial in London or more particularly the Scott Memorial on Edinburgh's Princes Street. Outshining all the monuments surrounding it, it has suffered greatly over the years and needs serious restoration. The Swithin Anderton monument is on the left. (*Authors' collection*)

Alfred Illingworth (1827–1907). Alfred's father Daniel Illingworth founded Bradford's largest spinning mill – Whetley Mills. Alfred and his brother Henry later became partners in the firm and both married daughters of Isaac Holden, another of Bradford's 'wool barons'. Alfred had political aspirations and became MP for Knaresborough in 1868, a position he held until 1874. As a strong Liberal he became MP for Bradford West from 1880 until 1895. He was invited into Gladstone's cabinet but as he held somewhat 'radical' views he declined the offer. One of his 'causes' was his opposition to British occupation of Egypt and his interests here may well have influenced his rather extravagant choice of tomb.

Alfred Illingworth died on 2 January 1907. The funeral was held on Saturday 5 January, and the procession from the family home at Daisy Hill to Girlington Baptist church was watched by many hundreds of associates and local people. Both Alfred and his wife were cremated at Scholemoor Cemetery, and their ashes were placed in urns within the monument.

It is worth pointing out that people had differing views on Alfred's contribution to Bradford life, particularly his employees.

On 7 January 1907, the *Yorkshire Daily Observer* commented: 'At a meeting of the work people of Messrs Daniel Illingworth and Sons held at Whetley Mills, Mr. C. Hartley referred in sympathetic terms to the death of Alfred Illingworth. He had sought to shorten the hours of labour and he had taken the greatest interest in the welfare of the working classes in general.'

One week later, however, the same reporter reported remarks made by Ben Tillett, a leading socialist and one of the founders of the Labour Party: 'He had heard with regret of the death of Mr. Alfred Illingworth. Mr. Illingworth represented a type of his class with great strenuousness and distinctness, but the system which makes men rich was built upon little children's energies and men and women's powers of health and strength in industries which crucified body and soul!'

The structure of Illingworth's tomb is often described as a tomb but is strictly speaking a 'mastaba'. This is best described as an underground room for burial with an area above in which to place offerings, in this case the urns containing their ashes. When it was first built the entrance was protected by a bronze door detailed with Egyptian carvings but, sadly, this was stolen many years ago. The sphinxes were the target of yet another robbery attempt some years later but the thieves abandoned their attempt after being disturbed. (*A. Sachs*)

The Alfred Illingworth monument. (*Don McPhee*)

William Cudworth, noted
historian of old Bradford.
(*A. Sachs*)

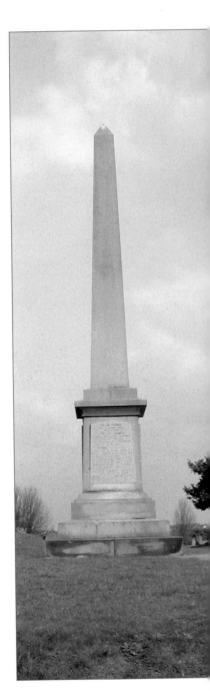

Joseph Smith (1801–58). The son of a Quaker family, Joseph Smith was born in Scholes, Cleckheaton. He soon became one of Bradford's leading luminaries following his move to the town in 1827. He laid out the Bradford–Eccleshill Turnpike and was heavily involved in many railway projects such as the Leeds–Halifax line in 1835. He became an alderman in 1847 when the town was granted borough status later that year, serving until 1853.

Joseph became the agent representing the cemetery company and was responsible for the sale of burial plots. He also drew up the plans to show where all the plots were. A major advantage of this job was to be able to choose the site of his own memorial and he chose well!

The obelisk he had designed by William Gay stands at the western end of the cemetery and is probably the most prominent memorial to be seen in Undercliffe. If you stand in the centre of the city today you can see Joseph Smith's monument way up on the hill, standing 33ft high and made of unpolished granite. A writer in the *Bradford Observer*, 14 May 1863, commented that the 'gigantic monolithic needle . . . for magnitude, beauty of outline, material and workmanship, surpasses anything we have seen in the cemeteries of England'.

Joseph Smith died on 22 April 1858 at the age of 57. William Cudworth, local Bradford historian, also buried in Undercliffe, wrote of Joseph Smith that he 'took a zealous interest in obtaining the Charter of Incorporation and occupied a conspicuous position in Bradford'. How true that was. Smith's obelisk is so prominent that until recently the Ordnance Survey used it as a permanent trigonometry point. What could be more fitting for a surveyor? (*Authors' collection*)

5

Mayors, Merchants & Others

Looking across to the large monuments flanking the main promenade at the unconsecrated end of the cemetery. The tallest is that of Robert Milligan.
(Authors' collection)

The butcher, the baker, the candlestick-maker, tinker, tailor, soldier, sailor, rich man, poor man, beggar man, etc., can all be found in the cemetery record of occupations. In one section within a few yards of each other are monuments to a veterinary surgeon, a picture-framer, a Wesleyan minister, a tallow manufacturer, a corn merchant and several wool-staplers. Elsewhere can be found a clogger, a sweep, a lamplighter, a soft-soap-maker, apothecaries – every trade and profession to be found in a thriving nineteenth-century town is there, and some that were not, such as a Turkish naval officer or a Ganges river pilot. Unfortunately we can only illustrate a few.

Robert Milligan, (1787–1862), first Mayor of Bradford. On his monument is this epitaph:

In memory of Robert Milligan of Acacia Road, Rawdon. Born in Scotland he became a resident in Bradford in 1808. His talents and industry guided by integrity and honour raised him to high distinction as a merchant. He was the first Mayor of Bradford in 1847. He represented the town in two successive parliaments with fidelity and distinction. He was generous and warm hearted in his hospitalities, liberal in his support of religious and other benevolent institutions. He departed this life in faith and hope of the gospel July 1 1862 aged 75.
  Also Phoebe (relict of the above)
  Born 25th November 1796 died 23rd of October 1868.' (*Bradford Libraries*)

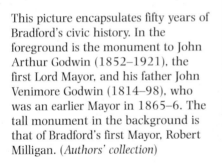

This picture encapsulates fifty years of Bradford's civic history. In the foreground is the monument to John Arthur Godwin (1852–1921), the first Lord Mayor, and his father John Venimore Godwin (1814–98), who was an earlier Mayor in 1865–6. The tall monument in the background is that of Bradford's first Mayor, Robert Milligan. (*Authors' collection*)

'Mayors' Row'. Here lie four of Bradford's early Mayors. When Bradford was granted its borough charter in 1847 it was able to elect a Mayor. The photograph shows, left to right, the monuments of Samuel Smith (1851–4), Robert Milligan (1847–8), Henry Brown (1856–9) and Joseph Farrar (1863–4). Joseph Farrar was a hatter, and a prime mover in the foundation of the Mechanics' Institute. (*Authors' collection*)

Besides his turn as Mayor, Henry Brown was the co-founder of the high-class Bradford department store, Brown, Muff & Co. on Market Street. His partner Mr Muff is in a grave not too far away. On 27 February 1878 Henry Brown laid the foundation stone of the new Dissenters' chapel in the cemetery. (*Authors' collection*)

Isaac Holden JP (1807–97). Born of humble parents in Paisley, he had a short career as a schoolmaster but then took the post of book-keeper at a Cullingworth wool-combing business (Townsend Bros). Becoming interested in the mechanics of the job he developed innovations in the combing process, but feeling he had not received sufficient recognition for his work he left and took out patents on his improved machines. Having joined up with Samuel Lister, they established a wool-combing business at various locations across France. As the business prospered he took his two sons, Angus and Edward, into partnership to become Isaac Holden & Sons. In 1864 he opened the huge Alston Works in Thornton Road, Bradford. A one-time Methodist lay-preacher in Cullingworth, he also became involved in politics, being elected MP for Knaresborough 1865–8, MP for West Riding division (North) 1882–5 and MP for Keighley 1885–95. He was made a baronet in 1893. Just before he died he became a Freeman of Keighley. (*Authors' collection*)

Sir Henry Mitchell. His tomb is in the form of a medieval shrine, made of grey granite. He lies alone. There are inscriptions to his family on the side panels but they are all interred elsewhere. (*Authors' collection*)

Above left: Samuel Smith (1805–7), dyer and Mayor (1851–4). *Above right:* Sir Henry Mitchell (1824–96). Born at Esholt near Bradford, he worked his way up through the textile industry where he had an illustrious career. He was the President of the Chamber of Commerce, a founder of the Bradford Technical College, and served as councillor, alderman and mayor (1874–5). He was made the first Freeman of the town in 1898 for his services to Bradford. (*Bradford Libraries*)

Angus Holden (1833–1912), Lord Holden of Alston, the elder son of Isaac Holden. At an early age he went to France and learnt the combing business at his father's works, later becoming a partner in the business. In 1860 he married Margaret Illingworth whose two brothers married his two sisters, thus uniting the two dynasties of Holden and Illingworth. It is not by chance that their respective graves and monuments in the 'elite' part of the cemetery are intermingled. Angus Holden had a distinguished political career, being Alderman, Mayor and Liberal MP for Bradford East. He was created Baron Alston in 1908. (*Bradford Libraries*)

Captains of industry, the Holdens and Illingworths. Sir Isaac Holden is seated in the centre. (*Bradford Libraries*)

Sir Jacob Behrens in later life. (*Bradford Libraries*)

The High School was built at the sole expense of Sir Jacob Behrens in 1862. He had been dissatisfied with the standards of the grammar school, and, finding the governors unwilling or unable to implement his recommendations, he financed his own school in Hallfield Road. Later, when the grammar school was improved, the pupils from the High School transferred there. Behrens also co-founded the Eye and Ear Hospital on Hallfield Road. (*Bradford Libraries*)

The Behrens monument is in the centre between the two obelisks. It is a fine neo-baroque memorial on the main promenade in the unconsecrated side of the cemetery. (*Authors' collection*)

A scrolled monument to Charles Rice (1820–80), the 'comedian' who was the lessee and manager from 1860 to 1880 of the Theatre Royal, Manningham Lane (now demolished). He seems to have been a man of many parts, writing plays and pantomimes, acting and even painting the scenery. The Theatre Royal was originally called the Royal Alexandra Theatre as there was an old, timber-built Theatre Royal in Duke Street. It was only after this was demolished that it was able to take that name. (*Authors' collection*)

The Theatre Royal in the early part of the twentieth century, long after the Charles Rice era. Obviously *Mr Manhattan* was a sell-out! (*Authors' collection*)

"Prince of Wales" Bradford Exhibition.
Aeronauts: R. Bramhall,   S. A. Smallbone.

Irvin Reuben Bramhall (1847–1929). A grave with a rather plain headstone was recently discovered to be that of a Bradford balloonist. During the Bradford Exhibition of 1904, held to mark the opening of the Cartwright Hall, I.R. Bramhall gave over 3,350 passengers an uplifting experience in his captive balloon. The opening ceremony was performed by the Prince and Princess of Wales, the future George VI and Queen Mary, who were on a visit to Bradford to unveil the statue of Queen Victoria at the bottom of Great Horton Road. (*Courtesy of the Graham Hall collection*)

Alfred Angus Scott, a pioneer motorcycle manufacturer, seen in 1923. He died of pneumonia after getting wet through pot-holing and then driving back from Malham in one of his own inventions, the 'Sociable', a three-wheeled open-topped machine. It was originally designed by Scott as a mobile gun-carrier in the First World War. (*Haynes Publishing Group*)

A detail of the Scott family memorial. In addition to Alfred's name there is a memorial inscription to Alfred's brother, Harold Wilfred Scott, who drowned at Salts Spring, British Columbia, in 1898. (*Authors' collection*)

Vintage Scott motorcycles in the cemetery marking the 75th anniversary of his death. (*Authors' collection*)

Thomas Shields (1832–87). Born in Scotland, he arrived in Bradford and founded the town's first daily newspaper, the *Bradford Daily Telegraph*, the forerunner of the *Telegraph & Argus*. He died after a long illness at the age of fifty-five on 27 October 1887. (*Telegraph & Argus*)

Thomas Shields's monument (centre) is a slender salmon-coloured granite obelisk in the unconsecrated eastern end of the promenade. (*Authors' collection*)

The gravestone of
William Rhodes, coach
proprietor (1799–1857).
(*Authors' collection*)

Detail from the gravestone of
John Totty, clogger of Bolton
Road (1822–71). (*Authors'
collection*)

Squire Pollard of Undercliffe (1823–67) was a keen cricketer. It's worth noting that 'Squire' was his first name, not his status! (*Authors' collection*)

Frank Burrows, champion roller-skater (1897–1959). As a keen pioneering motorcyclist he seriously injured his legs in a bad crash. His surgeon advised him to find a more sedentary pastime so he took up roller-skating! (*Authors' collection*)

6

Military Men

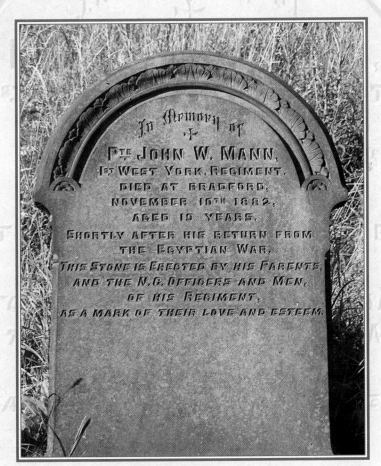

In Memory
of
Pte JOHN W. MANN,
1st WEST YORK, REGIMENT.
DIED AT BRADFORD,
NOVEMBER 16th 1882,
AGED 19 YEARS,
SHORTLY AFTER HIS RETURN FROM
THE EGYPTIAN WAR,
THIS STONE IS ERECTED BY HIS PARENTS,
AND THE N.C. OFFICERS AND MEN,
OF HIS REGIMENT,
AS A MARK OF THEIR LOVE AND ESTEEM.

Private John Mann. (*Authors' collection*)

In addition to the War Memorial (cenotaph) there are 134 registered war graves in Undercliffe. These are maintained by the Commonwealth War Graves Commission with the charity contracted to keep them tidy. All this work is undertaken by volunteers.

All arms of the services are represented, from both world wars. The casualties are those men, and one ATS girl, who died in the UK either from wounds received in action or through accidents. In addition there are many memorial inscriptions to servicemen who were killed overseas and were buried where they died.

The Commonwealth War Graves Commission is only responsible for the graves dating from the First World War and later. There are many military graves in Undercliffe recording soldiers who fought in earlier campaigns. These are just a few of the many Bradford men who lost their lives serving their country:

William Firth, died 1871: a Waterloo veteran;

Ellis Mann, died 1902, aged 79: he served on the North-West Frontier and in the siege of Delhi;

Pte John Ogden, died 1866, aged 36: 33rd Regiment Foot (Duke of Wellington's), wounded in the battle of Alma, Crimean War;

Lt Edward Coly Waud, died 1881 in Agrah, India: King's Own Dragoon Guards, memorial only;

Pte John Mann, died 1882, aged 19: 1st West Yorkshire Regiment, died following his return from the Egyptian war;

Harry Chambers, died 1900, aged 28: killed at Spion Kop, Natal, during the Boer War.

Opposite & above: The Cenotaph and two Second World War graves. (*Authors' collection*)

Matthew Hughes VC (1822–82). Private Matthew Hughes of the 7th Regiment (later the Royal Fusiliers) received his VC at the first investiture of the award in 1857 at Hyde Park, when Queen Victoria awarded the medal to sixty-two officers and men for acts of gallantry in the Crimean War. Matthew Hughes earned his decoration at the storming of the quarries at the Siege of Sebastopol, for twice bringing up ammunition under intense enemy fire. He then brought in a severely wounded soldier. A few days later he went out and rescued a wounded lieutenant, suffering a wound himself before returning to the lines. Referred to in the cemetery burial records as a 'beerhouse-keeper', his grave, marked only with a marker stone 'M. Hughes Owner', lay lost in the undergrowth. As a result of a campaign by S.J. Tidd, whose crusade in life was to find and commemorate the graves of 'lost' VCs, a new stone with a suitable inscription was donated by Russell Stone Ltd of Bradford at a civic ceremony attended by the Lord Mayor. The grave was rededicated by a canon of Ripon Cathedral. A guard of honour of Royal Fusiliers came up from their headquarters at the Tower of London for the occasion. Interestingly, Matthew Hughes had twenty-seven entries for misconduct in the regimental disciplinary book. (*Authors' collection*)

A bugler from the Royal Regiment of Fusiliers plays the 'Last Post' at the re-dedication ceremony on 11 March 1998. (*Authors' collection*)

The Essex Regiment. In 1887 a young soldier of the Essex Regiment died at Bradford Moor barracks; four more followed in 1888, three from the Essex Regiment and one Royal Engineer. They were probably victims of one of the epidemics prevalent at the time. The grave was purchased by the Regimental Sergeant Major, presumably from the proceeds of a barrack-room collection. (*Authors' collection*)

Bradford Moor Barracks. Built originally as a cavalry barracks it housed a number of regiments. After the Chartist risings of 1837 and 1840 the authorities thought it prudent to have a military force handy in case of further civil disorder in the town. Although the barracks were demolished many years ago the name lived on until recently with the nearby Barrack Tavern, now Habib's Indian Restaurant. (*Bradford Libraries*)

7

Tragedies

Robert Smith, the stationmaster who lost four sons in one week.
(*Authors' collection*)

There are many tragedies recorded on gravestones in Undercliffe Cemetery and sadly they are usually memorials to children. Look at the records and the list is endless.

Robert Smith, stationmaster at the Midland Railway station in Bradford in 1880, lost all four sons in the space of a week, victims of the scarlet fever epidemic.

There are the three Lumb brothers, Charles, 13, John, 9, and Fred, 6, who suffocated in the boiler room of All Saints' church, Little Horton, on 4 February 1871. Their father Jabez, the caretaker, was stoking the boiler when they crept in and hid themselves; he left unknowingly and locked them in. All were dead from the boiler fumes when it was realised what had happened. To compound the tragedy the father was dead two weeks later.

The first two days of 1883 saw the burials of 21 of the 54 victims of the Newlands Mill disaster. Many were children or teenagers. Most seem to have been buried in 'common graves' but the Boldy brothers, Joseph, 14, and George, 16, are in the family plot with a headstone recording the tragedy.

Fortunately not all were multiple deaths: there were many single fatalities, such as the drowning in 1875 at Filey Bay of ten-year-old Llewellyn Birchall. There were also families that lost child after child either through some then-unknown genetic fault or more usually because of then untreatable medical conditions. There are headstones which record the loss of five or six babies across consecutive years.

For many years over 80 per cent of burials in Undercliffe were stillborn babies or infants, most of whom were buried in company graves. Many were brought up to the cemetery on the tram and left at the office. However, the poorest stillborn child was recorded in the burial register along with the 'high and mighty'.

Adults too were not immune to misfortunes and untimely deaths. Fred Greenwood Smith lost his life in the tramway accident at Four Lane Ends (see p. 106). One of the most tragic was Pte Frank Dyson, Tyneside Irish Battalion, Northumberland Fusiliers, who was seriously wounded on the Western Front in 1918. He was shipped back to England but was killed when the ambulance carrying him to hospital collided with a tram.

In the days of Victoria's empire the sons of many Bradford families set off to find a better life in the colonies. Some went simply for adventure – anything was preferable to toiling in the 'dark satanic' mills. For many it was a fateful and final journey. As it was not easy to repatriate bodies in those days they were buried where they died. When families back home eventually learnt of their loss they would add an inscription on the family headstone so that they would at least have a focal point for their grief.

Drowning appears to have been a particular hazard during the days of Empire. Harold Wilfred Scott, 27, drowned at Salt Spring, British Columbia, in 1898. Frank Riley, 31, drowned in the sinking of the steamship *Zuetta* on the St Lawrence river in Canada in 1890. George Dixon, 33, drowned in the River Brisbane, Australia, in 1865. Charles Goldthorpe, 44, and Percy Clifford Averdieck, 22, were both lost in the wreck of the *Empress of Ireland* in the St Lawrence river, Canada. Goldthorpe, a woollen merchant, was brought back home and buried in Undercliffe. Some died on the long voyages and were buried at sea, such as Albert Hallfield, 20, who died while crossing the Indian Ocean in 1883.

The chimney disaster at Newlands Mill, Ripley Street, 28 December 1882. Of the fifty-four workers, mainly boys and girls, who were crushed to death, twenty-one were buried at Undercliffe. The youngest was eight years old. The illustration is a contemporary newspaper engraving. (*Authors' collection*)

The gravestone of Lavinia Cooper aged eighteen years, a victim of the mill chimney disaster. (*Authors' collection*)

Harold Wilfred Scott drowned in 1898 at Salt Spring, British Columbia, while returning from a wedding party on a neighbouring island. (*Authors' collection*)

8

A Victorian Funeral
& Cemetery Business

An illustration of an early Victorian funeral.
(*Authors' collection*)

As in most areas of Victorian life there was etiquette to be observed with the funeral. There was a 'correct' way for things to be done, for those who could afford it.

Mourning dress was mainly the preserve of women. If it was a husband who died then mourning dress could be worn for up to two years! A woman of high social standing would wear a black dress and a mantle with black crepe trimming on her dress. Her bonnet would also be covered with a crepe veil. Two years after her husband's death she could start to vary her colours with possibly grey or mauve. During the first year following her husband's death no social invitation could be accepted. After twelve months she could rejoin society. If the family was wealthy enough even the staff would wear mourning dress.

Mourning jewellery became popular during the Victorian period and in particular Whitby Jet, a fossilised type of wood, black and only found near Whitby in North Yorkshire. The jewellery was so much in demand that a whole industry built up in Whitby with over 200 workshops. Later on, less expensive 'black glass', also called French Jet, began to take over and the Whitby trade began to decline.

Ritual was paramount where the funeral was concerned. The funeral of Robert Milligan, the first Mayor of Bradford, shows to what extent this was taken. He died in 1862, and, as was the custom of the time for local dignitaries, shops and businesses closed for the day and crowds gathered along the processional route. His funeral was one of the most impressive held at Undercliffe.

The cortège was headed by representatives from the Bradford Corporation, the Board of Guardians and local magistrates. Friends of his, a number of policemen and the undertaker followed on foot. After them were several employees from the firm wearing black silk scarves. Three coaches contained his religious and medical advisers and the pall-bearers. The hearse came next, drawn by black-plumed horses,

Many of the Victorian and Edwardian funerals in Undercliffe Cemetery would have looked like this: see the description of Robert Milligan's procession – but he warranted six black horses to pull his hearse! Note the following carriage that is transporting the floral tributes. Some glass-sided horse-drawn hearses have survived and are occasionally used to this day. (*Authors' collection*)

and following were four more coaches carrying the male members of the family and friends. The procession was flanked by the local constabulary and followed by a large number of 'gentlemen' in their carriages. Behind all these 'official' mourners were a mixture of people known or patronised by Robert Milligan.

This procession ran from Milligan's home in Daisy Hill up to Undercliffe Cemetery where, following a long eulogy, Robert Milligan was finally and with all due ceremony laid to rest.

For the less well off, things were altogether different. There were 'funeral clubs' where one could save a little money regularly, maybe a few pennies a month. Families would have to borrow money or pawn items to avoid the ignominy of a pauper's burial. The body was laid out at home and family and friends would call to pay their last respects and to touch the body, which was seen at the time as an acceptable means of showing respect. The undertaker would then collect the body on the day of the funeral. A family member would in the meantime have visited the cemetery to arrange the burial details.

For those at the bottom of the social scale who could not afford a family plot, they would be unceremoniously buried in a 'company' or common grave. These did not have headstones or markers but all the relevant details were duly entered in the burial register – so there was at least a record that they had existed.

It can be instructive to study some of the surviving documents. For example, the Cemetery's Book of Rules and Charges states that Anglicans could only be buried from 3 p.m, Catholics and Nonconformists from 11 a.m. to 4 p.m. And in the Bradford Post Office Directory of 1883–4 there are listed sixty-eight stone and marble masons, forty undertakers and nine shroud-makers.

Furthermore, the Directors of the cemetery were quite adamant that no dogs should be allowed in the cemetery and they proclaimed sternly 'that smoking too was strictly prohibited'. Today, however, responsible dog walkers are welcomed as an

The last journey. (*Authors' collection*)

ongoing presence and a deterrent to mischief makers. In other words, extra eyes and ears!

The proprietors of the Bradford Cemetery were sticklers for rules and regulations as a letter from the cemetery manager to a certain stonemason makes clear: 'Sir I am informed by some of our men that while in the cemetery this afternoon at about three o'clock you were walking through the shrubbery amongst the trees on the terrace. Why you should do so I am at a loss to know. You will please "note" that there are walks provided for the public, by keeping to which, you will oblige.' One can only guess why the poor man had to go into the bushes!

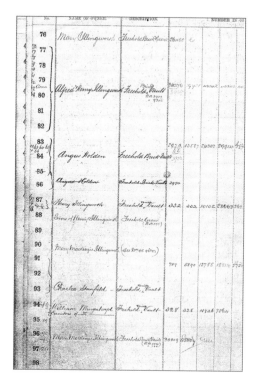

A page from the Register of Graves. The elite of society could afford to purchase multiple plots. Alfred Illingworth bought a row of six. He also bought the six behind and a further six behind those. This made a plot of eighteen first-class grave spaces. (*Authors' collection*)

By contrast the 'company' or common graves, for the poor who could not afford a family plot, held several dozen in the one plot. (*Authors' collection*)

Burial receipts from the Order Books. In 1865 the cost of buying a plot, having it dug and brick lined to take five burials and including the first interment cost £4 9s 6d. (*Authors' collection*)

By 1875 the cost of opening an earth grave and interment was £2 6s 6d. (*Authors' collection*)

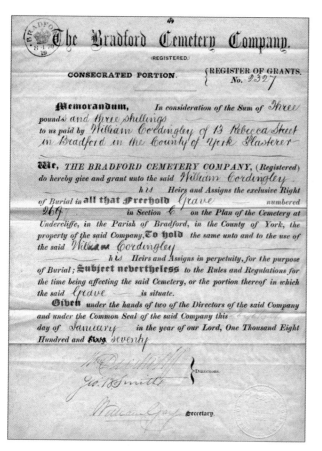

Grave grant of 1870 for Mr William Cordingley. Most people assumed that they had bought the land when they purchased a grave. This was not the case. What they had paid for was the right to be buried in that plot. Note the signature of William Gay, who by this time was Company Secretary. (*Authors' collection*)

Receipt for an obituary notice in the *Telegraph & Argus*. This is itemised on the undertakers' account. (*Authors' collection*)

Two undertakers' receipts for funerals that took place in Undercliffe Cemetery, one in 1884 and the other 39 years later in 1923. The Victorian one itemises an interesting entry for refreshments: three dozen buns and three bottles of wine. As there were two coaches and five cabs to transport the mourners, and assuming four persons per coach and two per cab, eighteen people attended. So everyone received two buns and one bottle of wine shared between six. (*Authors' collection*)

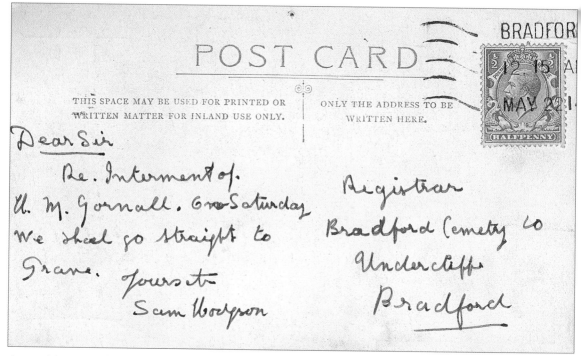

POST CARD

THIS SPACE MAY BE USED FOR PRINTED OR
WRITTEN MATTER FOR INLAND USE ONLY.

ONLY THE ADDRESS TO BE
WRITTEN HERE.

Dear Sir
    Re. Interment of.
U. M. Gornall. On Saturday
We shall go straight to
Grave. Yours etc
        Sam Hodgson

Registrar
Bradford Cemetry Co
Undercliffe
Bradford

A succinct message on the back of a postcard from Sam Hodgson, undertaker, cabinet maker and upholsterer, *c.* 1920. Joiners and cabinet makers made a natural and lucrative progression into the undertaking business, as did some drapers and cab proprietors. Eventually companies of specialist funeral directors took over the trade and were able to combine all the elements of arranging the burial. Sam Hodgson's building still stands on Carlisle Road, Bradford. (*Authors' collection*)

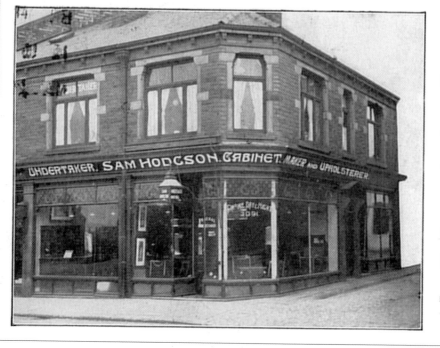

91 & 95,
Carlisle Road,
MANNINGHAM
(Opposite Free Library)

Telephone No. 2091.

FUNERALS
COMPLETELY
FURNISHED.

Attendance
DAY AND NIGHT.

BRADFORD CEMETERY.

NOTICE.

£2 REWARD.

Plants and Flowers having been Stolen at various times from the Graves and Vaults, the Directors of the Company offer the above Reward to any Person (other than an accomplice) giving to me such information as shall lead to the conviction of the Offenders.

BY ORDER,

JOHN THORNTON. Sec.

Stealing from graves is not exclusive to today's society. (*Authors' collection*)

HARRODS

HARRODS LTD

KNIGHTSBRIDGE
LONDON SW1

Telephone Sloane 1234 Telegrams "Everything Harrods London"

The Bradford Cemetery Co.,
    Undercliffe,
      Bradford,
        Yorks.

27th January 1937.

Ref. No. 252/37/S.

Dear Sirs,

    We understand that you are holding in reserve for Mr. Harold Smith, of Belle Vue, Sudbury Hill, Harrow-on-the-Hill, Middlesex, a grave space numbered A. 120 in your Undercliffe Cemetery.

    This grave will be required for three interments, the first, most probably, being for Mrs. Smith, whose death is expected to take place at any moment; but of course no definate time can yet be given.

    We should be glad if you will advise us when you require the purchase of the grave to be completed, and if the charge of £28. 5s. 0d. includes digging for three interments.

    As soon as you advise us that payment is required, we will send you a cheque.

            Yours faithfully,

            Harrods Ld

            FUNERAL DEPARTMENT.

An interesting letter from Harrods Funeral Department dated 27 January 1937. Mrs Jane Smith of Harrow duly obliged and was interred on 3 February. (*Authors' collection*)

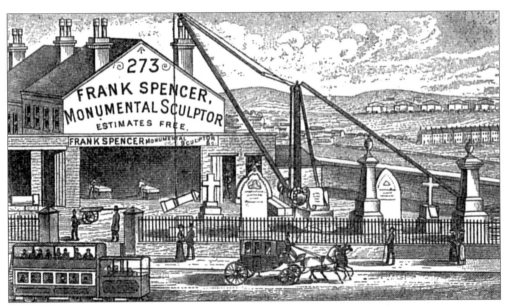

Enterprising monumental masons would always endeavour to obtain premises as near to the cemetery gates as possible. Frank Spencer's firm actively canvassed departing mourners after a funeral to increase business and undercut the Bradford Cemetery's 'in house' monumental service. A short and very explicit letter from the cemetery secretary put an end to this practice. Spencer's premises were eventually taken over by Wright & Sons Ltd, a firm that is still in the business. Frank Spencer is himself buried in Undercliffe Cemetery. This illustration depicts the transitional period in public transport in the late Victorian era, with horse power and a steam tram passing each other in Otley Road where there is still, inset in the cemetery wall, a water trough for the horses after their steep ascent from the town. (*Authors' collection*)

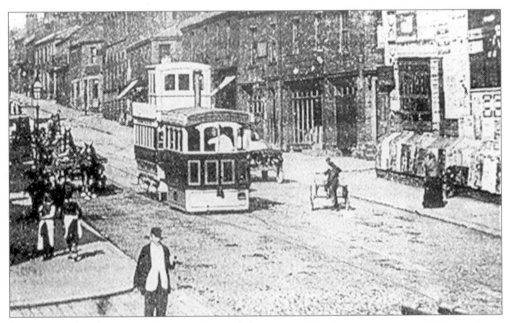

A tram on its way to town via East Parade. Visitors to the cemetery would have been transported up the hill to Undercliffe on this form of public transport. (*Bradford Libraries*)

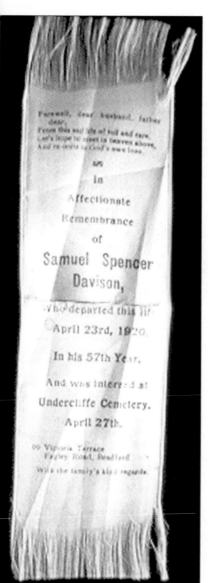

It was usual to hand out 'death cards' but this rather unusual memento mori was in the form of a printed silk ribbon, presumably a book mark. (*Authors' collection*)

Before the days of hydraulic lifting gear the Victorians were still using ancient technology to erect monuments. This old photograph, which is thought to have been taken in Scholemoor Cemetery, illustrates the method used. Horses would have been used for the lifting power. Note the missing rung on the ladder! (*Authors' collection*)

Masons' yard, *c.* 1900. This interesting photograph shows masons at work and the two 'gaffers'. Monumental masons and cutters (letterers) are becoming scarce today. Much of the lettering and cutting is now done by computers and lasers. (*Authors' collection*)

A rather grainy old photograph of the Bradford Cemetery's own masons' yard. This had been the farmhouse and outbuildings of earlier times when it was part of the Hustler estate. Note the crates. Many monuments arrived from the granite and marble quarries as ready to assemble sets. The masons then built them up and added the inscriptions. (*Authors' collection*)

The masons' yard, late 1940s. Alan Strudwick, second left, was the son of the Registrar. He was apprenticed to the master mason and learnt his trade at Undercliffe. (*Authors' collection*)

In Otley Road just below the cemetery Wm Wright & Sons had premises to display their goods. Some of those seen here would have found their place in Undercliffe Cemetery. (*Authors' collection*)

Wm Wright & Sons' display window. The bust of Queen Victoria was probably sold as a memento mori following her death in 1901. (*Authors' collection*)

The last Registrar to live in the Registrar's house at the cemetery was Thomas Ellis Strudwick. He is seen here with Mrs Strudwick and their grandson Neil. This photograph was taken in the back garden of the house. The site is now the car park at Undercliffe Lane. Mr Strudwick's last entry in the burial register was on 2 November 1969. Stonemason Herbert Naylor then officiated as Registrar and General Manager until the cemetery company went into liquidation in 1976. (*Authors' collection*)

The Bradford Cemetery Company had its own monumental masons and works. This was a lucrative part of the company's business, and although bereaved families could go to many monumental sculptors and masons for their memorial the majority seem to have opted for the 'in house' service. In addition to sample monuments in the entrance to the cemetery, advertising postcards such as those shown here and stock sample catalogues were used as sales aids. Even recent jobs were photographed to show prospective customers. On the back of this card written in pencil is '£22 as photo, with plain borders £20, flags and chippings £1–10s extra'.

The sexton's lodge. This stood opposite the Registrar's office at the Undercliffe Lane entrance. It became derelict after the Bradford Cemetery Company abandoned the site. The old grave-digger Billy Marriott would not move out even after the electricity and water had been cut off. (*Authors' collection*)

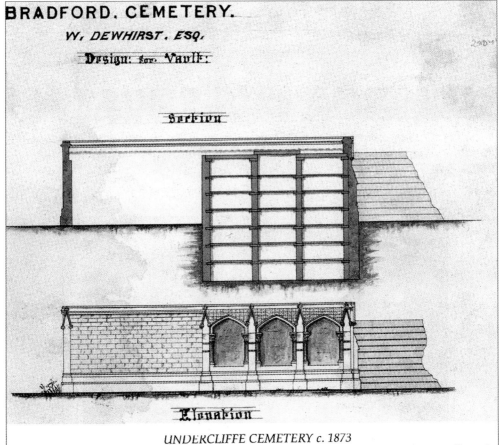

BRADFORD. CEMETERY.

W. DEWHIRST. ESQ.

Design: for Vault:

Section

Elevation

UNDERCLIFFE CEMETERY c. 1873
Design of a vault in Undercliffe Cemetery by William Gay for William Dewhirst, a local stuff mercha
William Dewhirst was actually interred in the vault ten years later, in 1883.

Opposite (below), above & right: William Dewhirst JP, a wealthy stuff merchant, commissioned William Gay to design this arcaded vault to take twenty-one interments. By the time he died in 1883 he had changed his mind and bought a huge plot on the central promenade, presumably to be with the other luminaries who were being buried there. The vault was sold on to three separate families. (*Opposite, below: West Yorkshire Archives; this page: Authors' collection*)

During the 1970s the late Alfred Robinson began the most comprehensive study of the monuments in Undercliffe Cemetery, and in particular the epitaphs upon them. He wrote in an article for the Bradford and Calderdale Chamber of Commerce in 1978 that the 'epitaphs on the memorials in Undercliffe Cemetery are in effect a history of Bradford inscribed in stone and marble'.

On a monument next to that of Robert Milligan is the tomb of Henry Brown, proprietor of Bradford's former well-known department store in Market Street (Brown Muff's). The grey granite monument has three polished panels with the following inscription:

> Born in Bradford on 8 November 1805, he spent his life here and by diligence, prudence and perseverance, acquired a competency more than sufficient for his simple wants. Loving the place of his birth, he strove to leave it better than he found it and devoted his time and energy in promoting its civic and social welfare.

Henry Brown was Mayor of Bradford three times in his lifetime and following his death in Brighton on 25 March 1878 he was laid to rest in Undercliffe 'in the presence of a large concourse of his fellow-townsmen'.

As would be expected most of the verses on these memorials are either direct biblical quotations or versions of them. There is however one notable exception and that is of William Sharp, fishmonger, who died on 7 April 1900, aged seventy. The inscription reads:

> The world is my country
> All mankind are my brethren
> And to do good is my religion.

This inscription is a corruption of Thomas Paine's *The Rights of Man*, which read 'My country is the world, and my religion is to do good.'

Some people used accurate verses to recall their life and one of these was Victor Hall who died in 1910. His inscription was from Edward Fitzgerald's translation of *The Rubaiyat of Omar Khayyam* and reads:

> Lo, some we loved, the loveliest and the best
> That time and fate of all their vintage prest,
> Have drunk their cup a round or two before,
> And one by one crept silently to rest.

One unusual and slightly amusing headstone is that of one David Brearley who died aged sixty-six in June 1860. The first thing to be pointed out is that he was a Druid! Slightly unusual, but what highlights this tombstone is the number of spelling mistakes; also the spacing of the letters leaves a lot to be desired.

Another unusual epitaph is that of Fred Greenwood Smith, aged twenty-nine, who 'lost his life in the tramway accident at Four Lane Ends, Girlington in December

'1889'. The accident was reported in the *Bradford Observer*. The fatality occurred at about 7 o'clock in the evening when car 21 belonging to the Bradford Tramways and Omnibus Co. Ltd detached itself and ran backwards down Allerton Road (passengers 'being naturally thrown into a state of the utmost consternation'), crossed over Thornton Road and overturned, not inappropriately in Cemetery Road!

Our thanks go to Mrs Alfred Robinson for permission to quote from her late husband's work.

Alfred Robinson, local historian, wrote many articles on his research among the tombstones but it is for his sterling work in saving the cemetery records that he is owed the greatest debt. (*Bradford Libraries*)

It was in this fire-damaged and vandalised Registrar's office that Mr Robinson and his colleague John Jackson worked tirelessly to collect the burial records and cemetery papers, which they placed in the safekeeping of the Bradford Archives Office. Without their efforts we would know virtually nothing. (*Authors' collection*)

A view through the vandalised cemetery office window – a view that Alfred Robinson would have been familiar with. (*Telegraph & Argus*)

The Wagstaff Barlow Memorial. One of the most poignant memorials is that of William Wagstaff Barlow, Registrar of Marriages for the Bradford Poor Law Union. It features a reclining lady with a baby in her arms but the marble from which it was carved has not stood the test of time and weather and it is now hard to make out the original lines. Also named on this memorial are William's first wife Anne who died aged thirty-three in 1867 and that of their daughter Sarah Elizabeth, who survived only a few weeks after her birth in 1859. It is assumed that these are the people depicted in the carving adorning the tomb. (*Authors' collection*)

9

Location, Location, Location

The twenty-first-century view of Bradford from the western end of the cemetery.
The tradition of using Undercliffe Cemetery for film and television productions started in
the 1960s with the classic film *Billy Liar*. This was before the years of abandonment and
neglect! As the site became more accessible film-makers flocked back eager to use the
dramatic atmosphere and gritty vistas of a Yorkshire landscape, encapsulating the feeling
of a northern funeral on a windswept hill. *Blood and Peaches, King Girl, Band of Gold,
LA Without a Map* and *Shipman* have all used the cemetery for their most dramatic
scenes. Many TV crews doing a piece to camera on a topical issue concerning Bradford
exploit the dramatic view of the city that they can obtain from the western end of the
site. (*Authors' collection*)

Right: A scene from *Billy Liar*. Tom Courtenay gets amorous with Helen Fraser. (*Vic Films*)

Left: Author Keith Waterhouse retraces the scenes from *Billy Liar*, filmed in the cemetery in the early 1960s. (*Authors' collection*)

Right: A film crew at work round the Smith obelisk. The monument immediately behind the actors is a film prop. (*Vic Films*)

The TV production company takes over the promenade and a Victorian hearse is brought in for a Mafia-style funeral in the *Secret World of Eddie Weary*, written by Roy Clarke, creator of *Last of the Summer Wine*. (*Authors' collection*)

In 1997 the cemetery became a film set for the Anglo-American production *LA Without a Map*, the story of a Bradford funeral director who meets an American girl in the cemetery and follows her back to the States looking for romance and fame. David Tennant and Vanessa Shaw meet in the cemetery. (*Dan Films*)

LA Without a Map, Scene 1, a funeral in a wintry northern cemetery. Local people were used as extras, including a Bradford councillor and the funeral director of a well-known local firm which also provided professional advice to the film crew. A cemetery volunteer doubled as the grave-digger. (*Dan Films*)

10

A Monumental Sight

The cemetery is an enchanting place in winter when the hoar frost or a light dusting of snow decorates the monuments. (*Authors' collection*)

Opposite & right: These two photographs illustrate two very different approaches to death. The self-assured ostentation of the upper-class Victorians, with everyone vying for status and recognition in death as they had in life, and the modest uniform Quaker burial ground. All the memorial stones are laid flat: 'no man is above another' is their philosophy. (*Authors' collection*)

Monuments garlanded with ivy can look picturesque but eventually it smothers the structure and has to be removed – time and time again! (*Authors' collection*)

View from the promenade looking down to the historic core, referred to in Victorian times as the 'select flat'. (*Authors' collection*)

Looking down the main concourse with the Smith obelisk as the focal point. The historic core is below the bank on the right. The two mortuary chapels were to the left. (*Authors' collection*)

A rustic cross silhouetted in the evening light, looking across the valley towards Manningham.
The cemetery is approximately 600ft above sea level. (*Authors' collection*)

The Garnett family owned Barker End Mills, Worsted Spinners, just down the road from the
cemetery. At one time they were connected with the Paper Hall at the top of Church Bank,
the oldest secular building in the city. (*Telegraph & Argus*)

The Holden family memorial on the promenade. This was built to house the remains of three members of the Holden family who were initially buried at Lille in France, where the Holdens owned mills. The monument is built from grey limestone, reputed to have been shipped from Belgium. (*Authors' collection*)

Detail of the Behrens memorial. The high status workmanship and baroque style of the monument suggests it would not be out of place on the façade of a Viennese palace. (*Authors' collection*)

The promenade, unconsecrated end. The first in line of these prominent monuments is that of John Steele, surgeon (1810–63), born in Edinburgh. It was erected by his fellow townsmen. (*Authors' collection*)

The weeping elm, sadly a victim of Dutch elm disease, had to be felled recently and is a great loss to the landscape. (*Richard Newman*)

The Four-poster. A Graeco-Roman temple-like structure where Eugenia Fanny Lassen lies at eternal rest. *(Don McPhee)*

The monument to Miles Moulson, stonemason (1806–56). *(Authors' collection)*

Opposite above: The Gazebo. This stands at the western end of the cemetery. It was installed at the time of the restoration programme as part of an aborted scheme for a garden of remembrance. However, it does make a fine subject for this photograph. *(Richard Newman)*

Opposite below: The full vista of Undercliffe's finest feature, the promenade, so nearly lost for ever a few years ago. It was described by the editor of the *Telegraph & Argus* as 'the jewel in Bradford's crown'. *(Authors' collection)*

Not all the memorials in Undercliffe Cemetery are the grand edifices of the wealthy Victorian and Edwardian upper classes. Many graves are unmarked and many later graves commemorated with a simple vase or wooden cross. As time went on the well-to-do saw less need for the elaborate monuments of their forefathers and ordinary folk were able to afford a modest gravestone. So the gulf between the well-off and those of more modest means evened out. (*Authors' collection*)

In 2001 cemetery volunteers arrived one morning to find a new monument. It was a substantial pyramid of large cobblestones that had been carried some distance and erected overnight near the Joseph Smith obelisk. A rudimentary inscription in white paint suggested that somebody had lost a friend and was attempting to immortalise him unofficially at this prominent spot. (*Authors' collection*)

A detail from the monument of
David Brearley, a boot and shoe-
maker . . . and Druid
(1794–1860). (*Authors' collection*)

A detail from the monument of Moses
Briggs, wool-stapler (1837–85).
(*Don McPhee*)

The Grieving Widow:
a detail from the
monument of Benjamin
Ferrand (1818–56),
wool-stapler *(J. Booth)*.

The Scottish Widow?
(Authors' collection)

West Yorkshire
Bradford
SE1734

ENGLISH HERITAGE

Undercliffe Cemetery
GD2820
II

SUMMARY OF HISTORIC INTEREST

Cemetery opened in 1854 which was designed by William Gay (1814–1893), and considered to be his finest work. The core of the site contains many grand nineteenth-century monuments, and has been described as 'one of the most striking achievements of Victorian funerary design' (Brooks, 1989).

CHRONOLOGY OF HISTORIC DEVELOPMENT

The Cemetery was established by the Bradford Company, which was provisionally registered in 1849. Representatives of the company, who included prominent Nonconformist businessmen Henry Brown, Titus Salt, Edward Ripley, and first Mayor of Bradford Robert Milligan, bought the land at Undercliffe in 1851 at a cost of £3,400. William Gay, who was appointed the first Registrar, laid out the site at a cost of £12,000. He subsequently designed a number of cemeteries, chiefly in the north of England, of which this is considered the most distinguished (Brooks 1994).

Plans were drawn up for the extension of the site to the west in 1876. These were never carried out but the proposal map includes the whole of the existing site and shows Gay's executed design. The Cemetery, which contains more than 23,000 graves and approximately 124,000 interments, including those of many notable figures of nineteenth-century Bradford, remains open for burials (1998).

The site was sold to a private owner during the 1970s and was bought by Bradford City Council in 1984; it is currently (1998) leased to The Undercliffe Cemetery Charity as a custodian of the site on behalf of the Local Authority.

SITE DESCRIPTION

LOCATION, AREA, BOUNDARIES, LANDFORM, SETTING

The Cemetery is situated on the north-east side of Bradford, c3km from the city centre. The c10ha site is on the crest of Undercliffe Hill, c210m above sea level. The land slopes down to the north and west, commanding long distance views of the city and the Pennines beyond. The boundaries are walled and are formed by Undercliffe Lane on the south side, Undercliffe Old Road on the east side, Otley Road on the north side, and by gardens of houses on Airedale Crescent and Airedale College Road on the west side. An area at the north-eastern corner of the site between Undercliffe Old Road and Otley Road is the site of a school, which replaced a stonemason's yard shown on the 1876 map, and is outside the registered area.

ENTRANCES AND APPROACHES

There are two main entrances, one on the south side of the site, on Undercliffe Lane, where there are rebuilt stone walls and gatepiers. A lodge and a Registrar's Office in this position were demolished during the 1970s. They have been replaced by a nineteenth-century stone lodge brought from another site and re-erected in the late twentieth century. The other entrance is on the north side of the site, on Otley Road. A lodge which stood at this entrance was also demolished in the 1970s, but the stone walls and gatepiers survive.

PRINCIPAL BUILDINGS

The principal buildings of the Cemetery were two chapels which were situated slightly to the east of the centre of the site, overlooking a promenade. These replaced chapels of 1854, and were designed in 1878 by Lockwood & Mawson. They were demolished during the 1980s and the foundations are visible c80m north of the Undercliffe Lane entrance.

OTHER LAND

The main axis of the Cemetery is a broad promenade which runs east/west along a spine of high ground for almost the whole length of the site, dividing it into two parts, the southern of which is slightly narrower than the northern. The promenade, which is lined with striking nineteenth-century monuments, is connected with the entrances by a system of straight and curving paths which conform with the layout shown on the 1876 map. The map also shows a line of planting dividing the more expensive plots along the south side of the promenade from cheaper ones further to the south. This has disappeared and the area is all in used as burial plots. A similar line of planting separated the plots along the northern side of the promenade from plots to the north, and elements of this survive. Views to the north are obtained from the whole of the promenade; at its west end the ground drops away steeply and there are long-distance views to the south-west, west and north. This is the site of an obelisk (listed grade II), c10m in height, which forms the termination of the vista, and is a memorial to Joseph Smith (d.1858) who was land agent to the Cemetery Company and reserved this plot for himself. c100m north-east of this is a roughly circular area, with the late twentieth-century circular openwork cast-iron structure at the centre, which was landscaped in the late twentieth century for use as a memorial garden, though the landscaping was not completed.

The focus of the site is slightly east of the centre, where the two chapels were situated on the south side of the promenade. The ground is terraced down on the north side of the promenade, and a set of stone steps, aligned midway between the two chapel sites, leads down the slope to a broad terrace on which an elliptical area, with quartering paths, is delineated by a perimeter path. A second set of stone steps, aligned with the first, leads down from the north side of this area and connects with winding paths from the Otley Road entrance. Plots in this central area, like those on each side of the promenade, were the most expensive, and they have a concentration of the largest and most ornate of the nineteenth-century monuments. Those listed grade II are the Mawson Monument and the Behrens Mausoleum within the central elliptical area, and the Miles Moulson Monument c80m to the north-east of this.

On the eastern side of the site, which was reserved for Nonconformist burials, there is an area of Quaker burials which is situated c110m north-east of the Undercliffe Lane entrance and is distinguished by the modest rectangular memorial stones, all of identical design and laid flat, which contrast with the ornate monuments of other parts of the site.

There are the remains of nineteenth century and later ornamental planting around the site perimeter, from which it has encroached as scrub.

The design for Undercliffe was probably inspired by Joseph Paxton's Coventry Cemetery of 1847 which incorporated an architectural terrace, and Gay's development of his idea may have influenced Edward Kemp, whose layout of Anfield Cemetery in Liverpool (q.v.) incorporates features such as a sunken elliptical area overlooked by a promenade and a system of curving paths.

The Cemetery Directors were conscious of the recreational possibilities of this site. In the 1850s they wrote: 'The situation of the Cemetery is one of great beauty, and the views of the surrounding country . . . are not to be surpassed in the neighbourhood of Bradford. Whilst it will be the endeavour of the Directors, to preserve the greatest possible decency and decorum, in the conduct of the interments, they also desire to throw the Cemetery open to the public as much as possible . . . and so long as propriety of behaviour is observed, none will be excluded from the grounds, who desire to avail themselves thereof, either as a place of relaxation or for contemplative retirement.' (in Beesley & James, 1991). The site became a 'favourite promenade of the inhabitants of Bradford' (*ibid.*) and an entraving of c1854 shows fashionably-dressed crowds walking in the Cemetery and pointing at the views of the city below.

REFERENCES

Published sources
N. Pevsner, *The Buildings of England: West Yorkshire.*
C. Brooks, *Mortal Remains*, 1989, pp58, 59, 64, 68, 89, 105, 127–8, 140, 142.
I. Beesley & D. James, *Undercliffe, Bradford's Historic Victorian Cemetery*, 1991.
C. Chapple, *Undercliffe Cemetery*, n.d., c1994.

ACKNOWLEDGEMENTS

The authors would like to thank the many people who have helped with the photographs, research and memorabilia that have gone into this book: the Undercliffe Cemetery Charity Committee, and particularly Ann Clark, the Cemetery Registrar; Peter Walker of Bradford Central Library, who helped with the photographs from the J.L Booth collection; Perry Austin-Clarke, editor of the Bradford *Telegraph & Argus* for permission to use photographs from the paper's archive; Bradford Art Galleries and Museums for the painting *Bradford View* by J.W. Anderson; Andrew George and his team at the West Yorkshire Archives.

Many photographers have recorded the various 'ups and downs' of the cemetery. Particular thanks go to Don McPhee of the *Guardian*; to Richard Newman and Mark Kilburn; to Mrs Alfred Robinson for permission to quote from her late husband's work; and to Jeff Clew, who provided the photograph of Alfred Scott on his bike taken from his book *The Scott Motorcycle* published by Haynes. Our thanks go to Graham Hall who provided the postcards of Undercliffe Cemetery and the Theatre Royal and who also helped to date some of the pictures.

We must also thank all those people who have simply handed over bits and pieces over the years that they thought would be of interest. Many have relatives buried at Undercliffe or have simply been visiting.

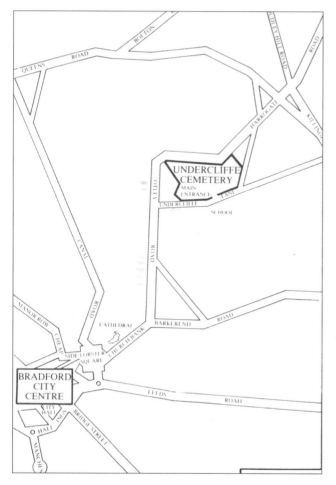